ABOUT THIS BOOK

While offering an abundance of cultural and natural experiences, England is still an insider tip for many. Together with Wales, it represents the lion's share of the United Kingdom, which also includes Scotland and Northern Ireland. The colonial legacy has made Britain perhaps the most cosmopolitan country in Europe, even though much is different in the island kingdom. Not only do the cars drive on the left side of the road, the days often begin with fried bacon, baked beans and eggs, and the pound continues to rule ok – in England past and future always live next to each other. The country is the cradle of modern democracy, yet it still holds on to the monarchy – except that the Queen no longer exercises any power. Nowhere else in Europe are there as many and powerful castles, palaces and cathedrals. The Beatles, the Rolling Stones and William Shakespeare, Agatha Christie, Charles Dickens

– English culture has long been a global culture. Nature also has much to offer, for example rolling hillsides, mysterious bogs and marshes, spectacular coastal cliffs and dreamy park landscapes. England and Wales are traditionally made up of 52 counties – based on historical units, these have today often been replaced by administrative counties. In the minds of the population, these old names are still common, especially since they are mostly identical with geographical names. This illustrated book takes you across all the counties and into all the large cities, revealing the diversity of the English and Welsh landscapes and natural spaces, as well as portraying the most important sights and regions worth exploring in more detail.

There are few other sights as archetypically 'English' as the typical red telephone booths – this one stands on a beach in Bournemouth in the county of Dorset. Although they have long been threatened with extinction thanks to the inexorable rise of the mobile phone, they are still preserved or repurposed, for example as miniature book exchange libraries.

CONTENTS

Above: The Lake District northwest of Manchester has preserved its mystique to this day – although at times England's largest national park has had to cope with very large numbers of visitors.

Pictures on the preceding pages:

p. 1: The guards in front of Buckingham Palace, wearing their typical red jackets and bearskin hats
pp. 2/3: The moated Leeds Castle, standing on an island in the River Len, in the county of Kent
pp. 4/5: You could imagine yourself transported into a fairy tale, yet although magical, Stow-on-the-Wold in the Cotswolds is quite real. The door, flanked by trees, belongs to St Edward's Church.
pp. 6/7: The distinctive dome of London's St Paul's Cathedral, with the Millennium Bridge in the foreground

CONTENTS

SOUTH EAST ENGLAND

The coastal landscape of South East England, running along the southern margins of the counties of Sussex and Kent, alternates between white chalk cliffs and pebble beaches, interspersed with famous seaside resorts like Brighton and Eastbourne. Further inland, the scenery shifts to enchanting green hills and idyllic gardens and parklands. Those wanting to trace back history will enjoy visiting attractions such as the moated Leeds Castle, picturesque towns like Canterbury, with its famous cathedral, and the cradle of Anglo-Saxon culture in Winchester.

St Margaret's Bay, named after the village of St Margaret's at Cliffe, is situated northeast of Dover, boasting two impressive cliffs – North and South Foreland – and beautiful gardens.

CANTERBURY

Canterbury has been at the heart of English church history right from the outset, and two World Heritage-listed religious sites attest to this early era: St Martin's Church outside the city centre, the oldest church in England still in use, dating back to the 4th century (or possibly even to the time of the Roman occupation); and the ruins of the Benedictine abbey founded in 597 by St Augustine, who converted the Britons to Christianity. The abbey ended up becoming the focal point of the newly created Bishopric of Canterbury. And it was in Canterbury Cathedral, whose initial construction in Norman style began in 1070, that Archbishop Thomas Becket was murdered by royalist knights in 1170. His gravesite there subsequently became a popular pilgrimage destination. Following a fire in 1174, the cathedral was rebuilt, bringing gothic architecture to England for the first time.

One of England's oldest cities, Canterbury is home to the head church of the Anglican faith (all pictures). The cathedral contains the gravesite of King Henry IV of England and Edward of Woodstock. It became famous as the scene of Archbishop Thomas Becket's murder. Becket was canonized in 1173.

DOVER

In prehistoric times, the coastal strip in the far southeast of England was connected to the continent of Europe. The only 'land connection' today, however, is the Channel Tunnel, through which high-speed trains from Folkestone, near Dover, zoom their way to Calais under the sea floor. When the sun is out, the chalk cliffs on either side of the port city of Dover gleam a radiant white, welcoming visitors who have cruised in from mainland Europe via the English Channel. Soaring up on the western side is Shakespeare's Cliff, featured in a scene of *King Lear*, while in the east towers the mighty Dover Castle. The limestone under the Norman fortress has been hewn into a maze of passageways dating back to the 13th century and Napoleonic times. These also doubled as Churchill's war rooms during the Battle of Britain in 1940.

Dover Castle (left and below, far left, top and bottom) was once considered the 'Key to England' because of its strategic location. The castle complex encompasses two natural cliffs that were banked up in the 11th century. Perched atop one is the actual castle, whose construction began in 1168, and on the other lie the ruins of a Roman lighthouse and the church of St Mary in Castro (built around 1000, large picture).

ROCHESTER

The city owes its importance to the strategic bridge over the Medway River, just before it flows out into the North Sea. The military and shipbuilding have played a key role here ever since Roman times. But Rochester is also the island's second oldest diocese after Canterbury. It was shaped by the Norman conquest of England in the 11th century, and indeed has the first Norman bishop, Gundulf, to thank for its impressive cathedral, which has managed to maintain its essential nature despite numerous destructions, reconstructions and extensions. Rochester Castle, one of the best preserved fortified tower complexes anywhere, is another typical example of Norman military architecture, while many buildings in the old town, such as the Guildhall, were erected in 1667 following a raid by the Dutch.

Rochester awakening to a spectacular dawn, with the cathedral and castle reflected in the Medway River (left). Rochester Cathedral (all pictures below) fuses three architectural styles: Norman, gothic and Romanesque – the latter being essentially evident in the stained-glass windows. The organ is a particularly imposing sight, colourfully ornate much like the side walls.

BODIAM CASTLE

When legendary comedians Monty Python satirized the Arthurian Legend and the English people's soft spot for the Middle Ages in Monty Python and the Holy Grail (1975), it was here that the 'knights' fought against the seemingly impenetrable walls. The moated castle, with its mighty towers, was built in the late 14th century, and was used more for representational purposes. From a military perspective, the battlements are much too flat, and even the pretty lake could be drained in a day. After its destruction during the English Civil War (1642–1651), the building soon began a new life as a picturesque ruin, immortalized in numerous paintings and repeatedly restored for this purpose. Today, it represents an 'ideal' medieval castle, attracting large numbers of visitors as if indeed by magic.

Bodiam Castle, completed in 1385 at the time of the Hundred Years' War between England and France, is well worth a visit. Watched by eight towers, the castle sits picturesquely in the middle of a lake. Despite its impenetrable appearance, however, it was to be homely for its noble residents, and builder Sir Edward Dalyngrigge designed it with 33 open fireplaces and 28 toilet recesses.

SOUTH DOWNS NATIONAL PARK

White is a colour nature reserves for the most special of moments – the ephemerality of sea spray, the transitoriness of snow, or the elixir that is salt. Only very rarely does it lend its pure hue to stone, making the impression all the more overwhelming when it does end up doing the full reveal on a grand scale. Mother Nature opens her heart the widest on the chalk cliffs of southern England, whose most spectacular section is found at the South Downs in Sussex and Hampshire. They rose out of a tropical sea aeons ago, and are made up of millions of compressed coral and crab skeletons, their flawlessness making them picture-perfect for eternity. But their beauty is fleeting. The rock is so soft that it cannot put up any resistance to wind or rain, and slowly sinks back into the sea.

One day, even the Seven Sisters, the most striking formation in the South Downs between Eastbourne and Seaford (both pictures), will become creatures of the sea once more, for the chalk is crumbling. Then, the only reminder of them will be the words of British writer Rudyard Kipling (1865–1936), who described them as 'Our blunt, bow-headed, whale-backed Downs'.

SOUTH DOWNS NATIONAL PARK: BEACHY HEAD

The captivating landscape of the Seven Sisters Country Park, named after the seven gleaming white chalk cliffs, begins just beyond Eastbourne. Following the coastline is the South Downs Way footpath, which runs along the top of the striking cliffs. The 163-metre (535 ft) Beachy Head, Great Britain's tallest chalk cliff, provides a breathtaking vista over the Channel and the famous 100-year-old Beachy Head Lighthouse in the sea.

The picture-postcard view of the Seven Sisters, however, is only visible from the next cliff, known as South Hill. This chalk cliff formation is located between Eastbourne and Seaford in the county of Sussex. The Seven Sisters are considered to be the most imposing chalk cliffs in the entire South Downs coastal region.

The Beachy Head Lighthouse (both pictures) has acted as a signpost for ships since 1902. And while it does protect skippers from the treacherous cliffs, it can do nothing to combat another tragic side of this headland: Beachy Head is where the highest number of suicides in Great Britain is recorded. A specially appointed team of counsellors watches the cliffs every day to make sure no one jumps into the depths.

BRIGHTON

In the mid-18th century, Dr Richard Russell wrote about the positive effect of seawater, namely in Brighton, on certain illnesses, resulting in the fishing town enjoying an unexpected surge in popularity. When, in 1786, King George IV ordered the construction of the Oriental-looking Royal Pavilion in Indian Mughal style with minarets, columns and a lavish interior, it all but ennobled the town, prompting more and more people to flock here.

Today, Brighton continues to be a popular destination for local recreation, in part due to its proximity to London. The city was once famous for its West Pier, built in 1899, but which was closed in 1975 and sadly destroyed by fire and storms in 2003. Plans to rebuild it have so far been unsuccessful. The i360 observation tower is a gigantic and therefore undisputed new attraction.

BRIGHTON

The famous royal seaside resort of Brighton, which boasts Regency architecture and once attracted members of London's glamorous high society, today continues to be a magnet for visitors. It is a mix of architectural styles, with the Oriental character of the Royal Pavilion (left) and the neoclassical Regency style of Brunswick Square (large picture). Far left top: Palace Pier, now known as Brighton Pier.

ARUNDEL CASTLE

This early-medieval castle, erected as a classic fortress on a mound of earth in the 11th century, is the stuff of fairytales. It has been home to numerous noble families, and has been extended and modified countless times over the centuries. Most impressive are its traditional towers, battlements and drawbridges, as well as its magnificent gardens, which provide the perfect setting for the cultural festival held here at the end of August, featuring a Shakespeare theatre, jousting tournament and historical re-enactments. The small town of Arundel is just as charming, welcoming its visitors with cobbled streets and meticulously restored buildings adorned with climbing roses and ivy. The attractive cafés and little boutique shops, meanwhile, are great places to recharge your batteries after admiring all the sights.

Fountains, lush greenery and stone structures provide a perfect setting for strolls through the gardens of Arundel Castle (below). But the castle itself (left) is also worth a visit. This sentiment was shared by Queen Victoria, who spent four days here with her husband, Prince Albert, in 1846 – a fact still proudly boasted to this day. Her bed, her bath and her guestbook entry are all available for public viewing.

ISLE OF WIGHT

A strait known as the Solent separates the Isle of Wight from the English mainland. The diamond-shaped island off the coast of Southampton is part of southern England's chalk cliff formations. And nowhere is this more apparent than at the southern tip, where the Needles continue the trail of chalk stacks rising up in the island's interior. The Isle of Wight is considered a mecca for watersport fans. Every August, sailing enthusiasts meet here in Cowes for the Commodores' Cup, before embarking on a one-week regatta. Every second year, the island also hosts the renowned Admiral's Cup race, which first set off from here in 1851. Eleven years prior, the Isle of Wight secured what is widely considered to be its most famous admirer in Queen Victoria, who, in search of a quiet, private country estate with her husband Prince Albert, had Osborne House built here in Italianate style.

Below: Osborne House is an authentic representation of royal life. The gardens surrounding the estate are always meticulously tended, boasting a vast array of colourful blooms all year round. Left: Alum Bay attracts geologists, as well as numerous other visitors, due to its sandy cliffs. Created by erosion, they glow in a wide range of different hues.

PORTSMOUTH

The port here has long been the most crucial base for the Royal Navy. And the old forts attest to its tremendous importance. Henry VII himself had Europe's first dry dock built here in the late 15th century, and it was also from Portsmouth that Admiral Nelson embarked on the legendary Battle of Trafalgar. His flagship, the HMS Victory, is today open to the public. Wharves and heavy industry later came to define the city, making it a target for German bombers during World War II. Despite this, Portsmouth was the departure point for the Allied troops bound for the D-Day landings in Normandy in June 1944. It took a long time for the city to recover from the war and structural changes. While only small sections of the old town were rebuilt, Portsmouth has a new, imposing landmark in the form of the 170-m- (560-ft-) high Spinnaker Tower, which was erected in 2005.

Portsmouth Port cuts a modern figure without neglecting its historic importance: The 170-m- (560-ft-) high Spinnaker Tower, designed by British architectural firm Scott Wilson and featuring a viewing platform, is intended to serve as a reminder of the city's maritime history (large picture). 'Spice Island Ghost Walks' are organized at dusk, in the historic Portsmouth Point district (below).

WINCHESTER

Built from 1079 to 1093, Winchester Cathedral attests to the construction boom to which England owes a number of new churches following the Norman Conquest (1066), and named after the English variety of the Romanesque style: Norman architecture. The crypt and northern transept have been preserved from this time. The arcades, the Triforium Gallery and clerestories in the nave – the longest in Europe, measuring 168 metres (550 ft) – and the retrochoir are considered characteristic of English church-building. The retrochoir, indeed, marked the start of the cathedral's conversion to the late gothic style, which gave preference to slender design elements. Fan vaulting was added to the central nave in the 14th century, during which the west façade, with its tracery and large window, was also created. Winchester Cathedral is famous for its artistically crafted chantry chapels.

Winchester was England's first capital city until 1066. Far left: The Great Hall of Winchester Castle with a statue of Queen Victoria. Below, far left, bottom: Guildhall (1871). The transept and spire have been preserved from the Norman cathedral (1079, below, far left top), while the main nave and choir in Perpendicular style date back to the 14th century (large picture).

JANE AUSTEN: ENGLAND'S FIRST FEMINIST?

In the end, everyone in Jane Austen's novels gets married. The confident Elizabeth Bennet gets the wealthy Mr Darcy; the over-indulged Emma Woodhouse marries the level-headed Mr Knightley; the sensible Elinor Dashwood ties the knot with her sister-in-law's brother Edward Ferrars; the withdrawn Anne Elliot weds her childhood sweetheart Captain Wentworth; the romantic Catherine Morland walks down the aisle with her cheeky young Henry Tillney; and the shy Fanny Price ends up with her cousin Edmund. Yet, unlike other, now forgotten female authors of her time, the Reverend's daughter from Hampshire took a highly sarcastic, clear-sighted look at the conventions, constraints and quirks of the landed gentry, the 'better society' of upper middle classes and lower aristocracy, before reaching her happy endings. The focus was on the need for women to find a good match to be provided for. Her heroines resist this, despite considerable pressure. This mix of love story and social critique was well received even during Austen's lifetime. Her sharp observations and elegant style indeed garnered praise from none other than Sir Walter Scott, the undisputed best-selling author of the time. Jane Austen herself never married, though she was fortunate to have come from a large, very well-read and tight-knit family.

JANE AUSTEN: ENGLAND'S FIRST FEMINIST?

Born in 1775, author Jane Austen spent her last eight years in Chawton, at the home of her sister Cassandra, before moving to Winchester shortly before her death. Austen died from kidney failure at the young age of 41 in 1817 and is buried at the cathedral. Jane Austen's House Museum in Chawton (left), a quaint little house and garden, opens up the writer's living quarters to visitors (large picture).

WINDSOR CASTLE

Windsor Castle, from which the British Royal Family takes its name, is not only Great Britain's largest castle, it is also the longest continuously inhabited one. A castle has stood on this site in the west of London for almost 1,000 years, first erected as a fort by William the Conqueror around 1070, and extended, modified, rebuilt and inhabited by English royalty ever since, including use as a fort, prison and garrison. The modern-day complex essentially dates back to the 14th century, when Edward III added the State Apartments, Round Tower and Norman Gate. The last major redesign occurred in the early 19th century under George IV. The castle today continues to be one of the four official royal residences along with Holyroodhouse in Edinburgh, Hillsborough Castle in Northern Ireland and Buckingham Palace in London, and is the preferred home of Queen Elizabeth II.

The flags and coats of arms of members of the Order of the Garter hang above the choir stalls, where each member has their own designated seat (left). The knights, in full regalia, meet in the castle and chapel every June; the Order is, after all, still the most prestigious in Europe. Below: a wonderful detail in the nave's ceiling.

OXFORD

Students dominate the townscape of Oxford, the home of Great Britain's oldest university, whose origins date back to the 12th century. The venerable colleges, the libraries with their precious stock – such as the Bodleian Library with its 4.5 million volumes, considered one of the world's most distinguished libraries –, and the prospect of good jobs are all motivating factors for students to take their lectures here. Oxford's towers, particularly Christ Church Cathedral's Tom Tower and Magdalen Tower, are visible from afar. It is worth paying a visit to the cathedral and the Christ Church Picture Gallery, which houses masterpieces from the Renaissance and baroque eras. Meanwhile, enjoy the view of the Radcliffe Camera building over a coffee and book at Blackwell's attractive bookshop.

The city centre is dominated by the 39 colleges with their distinguished libraries and chapels. All Souls College was founded in 1438, while the circular Radcliffe Camera building dates back to the 18th century, and is today a reading room (large picture). Below, far left, bottom: Hertford Bridge on New College Lane, which is also called the Bridge of Sighs due to its similarity to the original in Venice.

BLENHEIM PALACE

In 1704, the people of England gifted John Churchill, the first Duke of Marlborough, this magnificent residence in Oxfordshire as thanks for his successful crusade against French and Bavarian troops in the Battle of Blenheim (Blindheim on the Danube). Blenheim Palace was built between 1705 and 1722 under the supervision of one of England's most renowned architects, Sir John Vanbrugh (1664–1726). The three wings of the two-level baroque palace, with its towers and columned halls, were set around a large courtyard, and the sprawling gardens which were redesigned numerous times. The park created by Henry Wise, and modelled on Versailles, was renaturalized by landscape gardener Lancelot Brown in 1764, and transformed into a romantic setting comprising waterfalls and a lake to meet the demands and the taste of the time.

BLENHEIM PALACE

Blenheim Palace is one of the most impressive examples of baroque architecture in England. It stands amongst parklands designed to represent romanticist ideals. During the palace's construction, the duchess of Marlborough tried in vain to make architect Sir John Vanbrugh adopt a more manageable, homely design. Below: the Red Drawing Room with its numerous portraits of the aristocracy.

SOUTH WEST ENGLAND

Nowhere is England more diverse than in its south-west. The mysterious early civilization at Stonehenge, the Celts from Cornwall to Dorset, the medieval churches, the bustling ports and the seaside resorts make this region one of England's most popular. Coupled with this are the captivating natural landscapes all around. Quite lovely by the Severn and Avon rivers, and indeed Mediterranean on the warm south coast, they become barren and haunted in Dartmoor and Exmoor. In stark contrast are the spectacular steep cliffs with their bays and the wild Atlantic, which stretch as far as Land's End.

The small town of Sidmouth, situated in Devon, boasts a beautiful bay and an attractive beach. Despite numerous plans, Sidmouth has never had a port, most likely due to the fact that the bay could not provide enough shelter for a large port facility.

COTSWOLDS

The rolling green hills of the Cotswolds stretch across numerous counties from the southwest to the northeast. They are affectionately known as the 'Heart of England', and were awarded the title of Area of Outstanding Natural Beauty in 1966. This status is equivalent to a national park, and requires special landscape protection measures. The small towns of the Cotswolds are typified by their construction materials, for many buildings are made of golden limestone and covered in dark green moss. The beautiful 'wool churches' date back to the time when the wool industry brought prosperity to the region. Today, its affluence comes from the fact that wealthy Londoners and even many celebrities have their second homes in the lush Cotswolds.

Left: The Romans settled in Bourton-on-the-Water, though most buildings only date back to the 17th century, constructed from the typical Cotswolds stone, with charming gables and similar decorative features. Far left: Snowshill. Large picture: Lower Slaughter is a typically quaint Cotswolds village. Below, far left, top: Broadway Tower is 16 m tall (53 ft); bottom: authentic Cotswolds character in Bibury.

PASTIES, PASTRIES AND PIES

While the British are not exactly famous for their bread, it's a different story when it comes to their pastries. These can be made from shortcrust, puff pastry or choux pastry, and can have sweet or savoury fillings. And it is indeed all about the filling for British pies. Even in the sweet varieties, the dough is usually unsweetened, but very rich. This base is then topped with fruit – such as apples, blueberries, cherries or rhubarb – or nut and syrup mixtures, and then baked. Lemon meringue pie, made from lemon curd and beaten egg whites, is a popular treat in England, while mince pies, filled with minced dried fruit and spices, are usually only eaten at Christmas. – Steak and kidney, chicken and mushroom, chicken and leek, pork, and fish are among the most common savoury pie fillings. Stargazy pies, a curious Cornish speciality, even have the heads of baked sardines peeping out from under the crusty top. The most famous pasty also comes from Cornwall. The Cornish pasty is a half-moon-shaped pastry pocket filled with beef, potatoes, onions and swede, and originally a simple meal given to miners. Today, pasty stalls sell pasties with all kinds of unusual fillings, including Indian curry, spinach and walnut.

The most famous would have to be the Cornish pasty, which is sold on every street corner in Cornwall (left). Also well known, however, are Melton Mowbray pork pies (below, bottom) – cold pastries filled with chopped rather than minced pork. And the people of southern England love their sweet pastries too (below, top), with hot cross buns being popular gifts at Easter (large picture).

GLOUCESTER

The Roman settlement established on the banks of the Severn long owed much of its development to the port and the last bridge before the river mouth. The city was easily accessible from both the sea and the river, and later also via a tide-independent canal. St Peter's Abbey was founded as early as 679, and underwent substantial extensions during Norman times. Edward II, an unpopular king during his lifetime, is buried here. The monks were skilfully able to market his grave site as a pilgrimage destination, and the plentiful income resulting from this was used to redesign the abbey with superb glass windows – including the oldest depiction of golf as a sport – and delicate fan struts. The late gothic Perpendicular style remained the standard in English church-building for over 100 years. And if the ornate cloisters look familiar, it's because scenes from three Harry Potter movies were filmed here.

The Norman architectural style meets Gothic at St Peter's Cathedral in Gloucester. The large stained-glass windows in the chancel (large picture) and cloister (below, bottom) are particularly attractive, while the painted pipes on the organ (below, top) are also an unusual feature. In downtown Gloucester, Victorian warehouses line the docks (left).

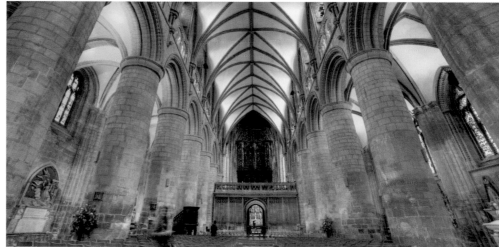

STONEHENGE

The British Isles' most famous prehistoric site has also been listed by UNESCO as a place of World Cultural Heritage. Stonehenge is said to have been built by Beaker folk in four stages between the years 3100 and 1500 BC. And the incredible structural feats achieved by this Neolithic people – they transported eighty-two gigantic bluestones here, presumably by river and over land, from the Welsh mountains – continue to inspire awe to this day. The bluestones were then replaced with 7-m- (23-ft-) high sandstone blocks at the start of the Bronze Age. The site has been modified on numerous occasions. Today, two concentric circles of stones sit at its heart, while seventeen trilithons and two upright monoliths with a transverse stone form the outer circle, spanning a diameter of 30 m (98 ft).

Debate continues as to whether Stonehenge (below) was used as a place of worship, an observatory or as a means of watching the sun. During the summer solstice, the sun rises precisely over the Heel Stone in line with the entrance path (far left). The remains of three other stone circles (left) are scattered across an area spanning 15 ha (37 acres) in and around the village of Avebury in Wiltshire near Bath.

SALISBURY

No matter the direction from which the city is approached, the mighty crossing tower of the gothic cathedral is visible from afar. At 123 m (404 ft), it is the tallest in the country, offering spectacular views of Wiltshire's farming landscapes. The old town, with its historic inns and half-timbered houses, also attracts many visitors. Yet Salisbury is a planned re-establishment of an older predecessor. By the 13th century, the fortified town of Old Sarum, which was located 3 km (2 miles) to the north and had been inhabited since antiquity, had finally became too small. This prompted local bishop Richard Poore to build a new cathedral on the River Avon, a step which ultimately resulted in the entire city being relocated. It is thus well worth making a quick stop to the picturesque Old Sarum hill, with the foundations of the fort and old cathedral.

The city of Salisbury not only boasts the nearby iconic site of Stonehenge, but also has much to offer in its own right, not least the 13th-century cathedral built in the pure Early English style (pictures below), with its 123-m- (404-ft-) high tower. The nave, with its column shafts made of dark marble, contrasts richly against the pale limestone of the side walls (large picture).

JURASSIC COAST

The Jurassic Coast, the name given to the spectacular coastal strip between Dorset and East Devon, sees deposits from the Triassic, Jurassic and Cretaceous periods on display like an open sandwich. The rocks are stony evidence of evolution, of the appearance and disappearance of flora and fauna, and not least of the dinosaurs. A species of dinosaur which only existed in this very location was discovered in 2000. Geologists were first alerted to it in the early 19th century through an accidental discovery by a little girl who said she saw a dragon on the coast. This was in fact the first complete set of prints of an ichthyosaurus. To this day, local hikers continue to find traces of prehistoric times here, with erosion constantly exposing new fossils, particularly after violent storms.

It is here that unique geological jewels lie buried: the Jurassic Coast (below) in southern England – one of the most prominent fossil discovery sites in the world, and a UNESCO World Heritage site since 2001 – formed some 185 million years ago. Durdle Door (left and panorama pages) is a natural rock gate.

BRISTOL

The largest city in South West England lies at the mouth of the Avon River, and shines resplendent in the vibrant charm afforded it by the port and universities. It has been a place of trade right from early times – with Ireland and later also North America, generating sizeable sums through the slave trade. Daniel Defoe found inspiration here for Robinson Crusoe after talking with sailor Alexander Selkirk. The wealthy Knights Templar have also left a mark on Bristol. The historic centre was destroyed on numerous occasions, most recently in World War II, as evidenced by a park filled with ruins, including those of the Temple Church. Many buildings have been meticulously reconstructed. And for the last few years, one of the most popular characters of our time has been turning his fellow residents' lives upside down at Aardman Studios. He is none other than Shaun the Sheep.

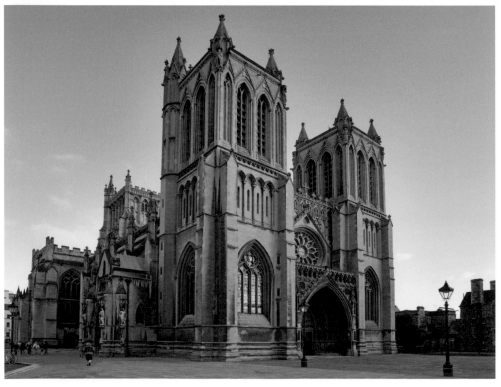

Large picture: Located on the southern side of the College Green, Bristol's library building was constructed by Charles Holden in 1906. Below, far left, top: Bristol Temple Meads is not only Bristol's largest train station, but also one of the oldest in the world; bottom: Bristol Cathedral is defined by its tracery windows. Left: Amphitheatre and Waterfront Square.

CLIFTON SUSPENSION BRIDGE

One of England's finest technical monuments is situated in Clifton, on the outskirts of Bristol. The wrought-iron suspension bridge has crossed the Avon Gorge since 1864. With its mighty towers and a span length of 214 m (702 ft), it was the longest of its time, devised and designed by engineer Isambard Kingdom Brunel. The high regard in which this technical pioneer – particularly of shipbuilding and railway construction – continues to be held to this day is evidenced by the fact that Brunel was ranked second behind Winston Churchill in a 2002 BBC poll on the top 100 greatest Britons. The spectacular views from his bridge are easily explored on foot, though the bridge itself remains a standard tollway. Four members of Oxford University's Dangerous Sports Club had something entirely different in mind in 1979, when they organized the world's first-ever bungee jump here.

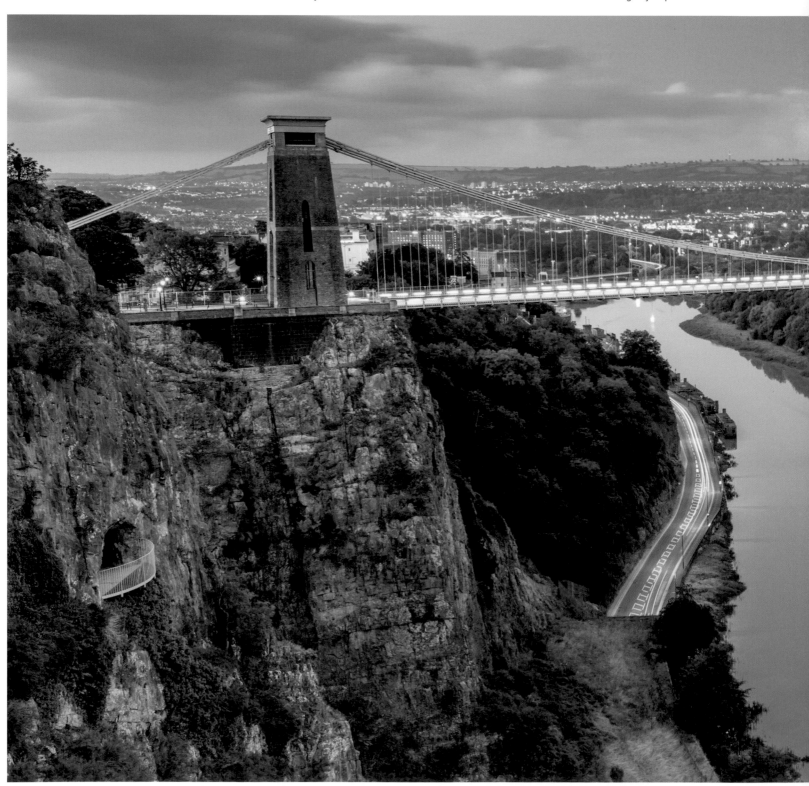

A visit to the Clifton Suspension Bridge requires a head for heights. Sadly, the bridge has also been a magnet for would-be suiciders. Twenty-two-year-old Sarah Ann Henley was in luck in 1885 when, attempting to end her life by jumping off the bridge, her skirt puffed up like a parachute and enabled her to land gently. She went on to live to the age of eighty-five.

BATH

Bath is located in the county of Somerset, not far from Bristol. And it was the Romans who established spa facilities and baths near the hot thermal springs. The city was previously known as Aquae Sulis, and remains of a temple and bathing complex today continue to attest to its tradition as a place of recreation and recovery. Having been a bishop's see and centre of the medieval cloth trade since the 10th century, Bath became England's most popular bathing town and the most prominent social centre outside London in the 17th century. It was primarily thanks to the monumental construction projects of architects John Wood, Ralph Allen and Richard Beau Nash in the late 18th century that the city acquired its compact Georgian townscape. Residential streets lead to classicist masterpieces like the Roman Baths, the Royal Crescent and the Pulteney Bridge, designed in 1770.

The city with the most elegant buildings in southern England is evidence of its architects' creativity. It is like a giant open-air museum for visitors. Bath is considered an example of the shift away from strictly geometrically planned Renaissance cities, and demonstrates how architecture can be connected with the landscapes surrounding it. Below: Roman baths; far left: Pulteney Bridge; left: Bath Abbey.

CHEDDAR GORGE

Not only has the small town of Cheddar in Somerset given its name to England's favourite cheese, but it is also home to one of the kingdom's seven natural wonders. A wild gorge with walls up to 113 m (371 ft) high and striking limestone formations extends for almost 5 km (3 miles). It was formed after the last Ice Age, when subterranean rivers created countless caves here. The almost 9000-year-old Cheddar Man, the oldest fully pre-served skeleton in Britain, was discovered here in 1903 in Gough's Cave, which had been inhabited for millennia. Studies of even older bones indicate the early dwellers were cannibals. The vibrant hues of the stalactite caves are a particularly popular attraction. Those interested can be whisked away into a fantasy world of lighting effects and video projections in Cox's Cave.

Cheddar Gorge glows a soft green at sunset (below). Left: Cheddar Gorge is home to several caves, including Cox's Cave, which was discovered by accident in 1837. The very next year, the discoverer turned the cave into a tourist attraction, even though not all of the subterranean chambers and passageways had been explored at the time.

WELLS

Wells owes its status as a cathedral city to its early gothic cathedral (built around 1180–1338). While the low side towers on the western façade make the building seem wider than its actual 49-m- (161-ft-) breadth, the some 300 stone statues give it a highly delicate overall appearance. The nave and chancel, both with three aisles and around 110 m (361 ft) in length, are each crossed by a transept. The chancel (built from around 1290 to 1340) is a masterpiece of the English high gothic Decorated style. It was extended by a retroquire and the octagonal Lady Chapel in the 14th century. The cloister, two-level chapter house and crossing tower also date back to this time. The master builders came up with a great way of supporting said crossing tower: they connected the crossing columns with pairs of mighty tapering scissor arches.

St Andrew's (large picture), the early master-piece of English Gothic (12th-14th century), is famous for its imposing scissor arches (1338) which support the crossing tower and give the cathedral a pronounced feeling of brightness and airiness (pictures below). The arches sit atop cross-shaped pillars. Left: The allegedly oldest residential street in England, Vicars' Close, is also located in Wells.

GLASTONBURY

The A39 coastal road heads inland at Bridgwater and continues onto Glastonbury, a place of myths and legends attracting countless mystics. There are several reasons for this high concentration of all things paranormal here: The remains of King Arthur – and perhaps even his Holy Grail – are said to lie under the ruins of Glastonbury Abbey, with its curious, solitary tower; Glastonbury is also believed to be the fantasy land of Avalon. Historic docu-ments attest to the founding of the first minster in the 7th century, construction of England's largest abbey church around 1000, and the dissolution of the monastery in 1539. The city is also known nationwide for its annual rock festival held here every June for midsummer, where mystics, rock fans and hippies pitch their tents – undeterred by the often rainy weather.

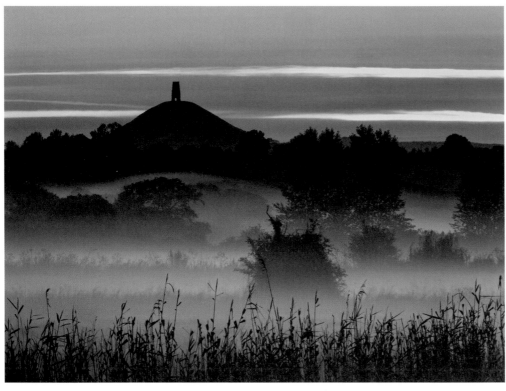

Below, far left: Mud and music – that's what the Glastonbury Festival is all about. It began during the hippy era, its first edition being held on a farm in 1970. Visitor numbers have grown exponentially, and the festival has become internationally famed. Large picture: The lights of Glastonbury and the starry sky outdoing themselves in the twinkling stakes at Glastonbury Tor.

EXMOOR NATIONAL PARK

There are grim tales to be told in Exmoor; tales like that of the executioner who was himself hanged: A hapless sheep thief who, high atop a cliff, flung a rope around his neck to seize his prey – and subsequently strangled himself. Those who travel to this plateau in the counties of Devon and Somerset will immediately understand why such tales exist; it is a harsh landscape of treeless moorland and plunging valleys through which the wind cuts with the sharpness of a thousand swords. The seclusion and desolate vastness perhaps also play a role in the mini horror stories that emerge from this region. One thing that most certainly does not contribute, however, is the Exmoor pony, the oldest pony breed in Britain, which can occasionally be seen roaming the area, and which is more reminiscent of something from a young child's fantasy than ghost stories.

Pale blue water, pink heather in bloom, and dark green grass make Exmoor National Park (pictures below) more vibrant than its bleak legends suggest. Gorse, ferns and hawthorn trees add dabs of colour to England's largest continuous moorland. Lynton, one of the larger towns in the area, marks the start of a coastal path along the top of the high cliffs (left).

EXETER

There's no room for understatement when it comes to the magnificent St Peter's Cathedral in Exeter, built on the foundations of a Norman predecessor church in the 13th century. The western façade is ornate enough in itself, but once you step inside, you almost have to catch your breath. The more than 90-m- (295-ft-) long arched roof of the nave, the longest of its kind anywhere in the world, is like a boulevard turned to stone. The cathedral is lavishly decorated, most notably with an astronomical clock that displays the time and position of the sun, as well as the phases of the moon with a silver ball. Equally impressive is the 18-m- (59-ft-) high, elaborately carved wooden bishop's throne, made without the use of a single nail, and instead held together by mortice and tenon joints.

The skyline of the diocesan town of Exeter is dominated by St Peter's Cathedral, built in the decorated gothic style between the 11th and 14th centuries. England's largest preserved group of sculptures, dating back to the 14th century, adorns the western façade, with its angels, queens and apostles. The ornate interior features an impressive vaulted ceiling (large picture).

DARTMOOR NATIONAL PARK

The 945-sq-km (365-sq-miles) Dartmoor National Park is a largely untouched woodland and moorland region on the southwest coast of England. It is situated almost 500 m (1,640 ft) above sea level, and is one of Europe's largest national parks. Dartmoor is not a primordial landscape; it has been cultivated for millennia. Numerous archaeological sites – remains of Stone Age villages, stone avenues and circles, monuments and burial sites – all attest to its long history of settlement. An approximately 800-km (500 miles) network of hiking trails criss-crosses the landscape, where, in some parts, solid granite outcrops, known as 'tors', soar out of the ground. Russet fronds, heather, windblown saplings and shaggy Dartmoor ponies typify vast areas of the national park's scenery, particularly in the barren west.

Large picture: The Great Staple Tor rock formation, which provides a spectacular view of the Merrivale Valley. Below, far left, top: A hike takes visitors up to Birch Tor, which offers an amazing view of the moor; bottom: Hisley Bridge above the River Bovey; the enchanted Wistman's Wood. Left: Evidence of the Bronze Age: The Nine Maidens stone circle near Belstone Tor.

TINTAGEL

Shrouded in legend, the ruins on Tintagel Head are considered to be the birthplace of King Arthur. Beyond the small town of Tintagel, a path leads over the cliffs to a lush hilltop in the Atlantic, surrounded by crumbling walls and accessed via a steep staircase. Excavations have found that, in the 5th century, this was the site of a Celtic monastery, home to a library, chapel, guesthouse, refectory and bathhouses. The castle, whose ruins can still be seen today, dates back to the 13th century, making the speculation about the birthplace of the mythical British king somewhat questionable. But anyone who stands high atop the cliffs on a misty day and looks down at the wind-whipped waves and the gaping cavern of Merlin's Cave may indeed feel they have been transported back to the times of King Arthur.

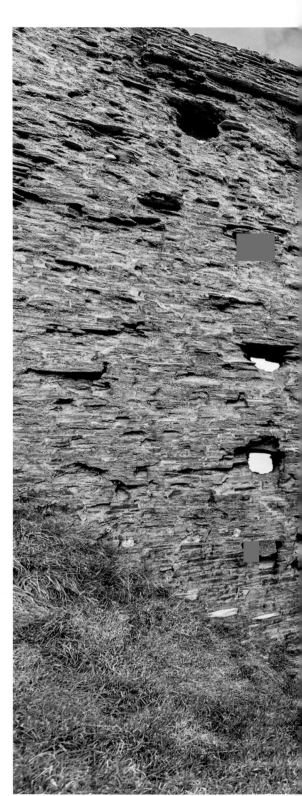

A place for storytelling. Whether or not the legends about King Arthur are true, the ruins right by the sea are always impressive (pictures below). Far left: Not far from Tintagel's ruins stands St Materiana's Church, serving as a place of prayer and worship just as it did in bygone times. It is presumed to have been built in the 11th or early 12th century, replacing an older church on the same site.

THE MINES OF CORNWALL AND WEST DEVON

Two-thirds of the world's mined copper in the 19th century came from southern England. From 1700 to 1914, Cornwall's economy, along with its landscape and social structure, was crucially impacted by mining. In 2006 UNESCO recognized this region and its history by including it in its list of World Heritage sites. The sale of copper, just like that of the tin and arsenic similarly mined here, required a good infrastructure, and trams, canals, railways and ports all attest to the early industrialization of Devon and Cornwall. In addition to machinery and structural remains of the mines, manor houses and working-class towns with beautiful gardens have also been preserved here. As several companies were involved in copper mining, and the quality of the copper deposits differed depending on the location, various technical processes were developed and used. With the establishment of the mines came the building of of small towns, with smelting plants and the typical terraced houses. The World Heritage site today covers ten different mining areas: St Just, St Agnes, Tregonning and Gwinear, Camborne and Redruth, Wendron, Gwennap with Kennall Vale and Devoran and Perran Foundry, Luxulyan Valley with Charlestown, Caradon, Tamar Valley with Tavistock, and the Port of Hayle.

The Botallack Mine complex is located in Cornwall's St Just mining area. It encompasses several smaller mines and shafts, including the Crowns Mine (left). The Wheal Peevor Mine, just under 2 km (1 mile) from Redruth, was closed in 1887 (below). Today, only the remains of three powerhouses and a few pumps are preserved for the public to see.

ST MICHAEL'S MOUNT

Perched proudly atop a granite island just outside Penzance in St Michael's Bay is the old castle of St Michael's Mount. Legend has it that the Archangel Michael appeared before fishermen on the cliffs above the sea in AD 495. From then on, the rugged little island in western Cornwall was named St Michael's Mount, and a church was built on it. The former Benedictine monastery was taken into the possession of the throne in 1535 and converted into a fortress. Historians date the monastery's founding as occurring in the 8th century. At that time, Celtic monks erected a monastery on Mont Saint-Michel in France, which looks astonishingly similar to its counterpart in Cornwall. At low tide, the bay can be crossed on foot; boats operate the rest of the time. The 70-m- (230-ft-) high rocky outcrop rewards climbers with a view of the Penwith Peninsula.

Due to its striking resemblance to Mont Saint-Michel, the small island off the coast of Penzance was most likely named after its original French counterpart. The legend of the apparition of St Michael probably did not emerge until later, also based on the French example. Left and below: Picturesque views of the monastery at sunset from St Michael's Bay.

ST IVES

Cornwall is today primarily associated with beaches and seaside holidays – and tourism is also the main source of income for the artists' town of St Ives, where the Romantic painter J.M.W. Turner praised the unique light. Grey granite houses characterize this former fishing village, which is home to one of Cornwall's finest beaches. Fascinated by the light and landscape, numerous painters and sculptors have been coming to St Ives since the last century. The Tate Gallery has now opened a museum high above Porthmeor Beach in the north, showcasing the work of local St Ives artists, including Patrick Heron and Ben Nicholson, who lived here with his wife, artist Barbara Hepworth. Ornithologists scour the region for rare guests like thrushes, warblers and vireos, who have lost their way and have been carried here by the westerly wind from America.

Scattered rocks and small islands lie off the coast of Cornwall; lighthouses like the one on Godrevy Island (right) are another common sight. Far right: Porthmeor Beach in St Ives.

LAND'S END

The westernmost point in England is characterized by an open landscape of heaths and moors brimming with archaeological sites: Tombs from the Ice and Bronze Ages, stone circles, Celtic crosses, and entire villages from the time before Christ all attest to a settlement history spanning millennia. The surging waves of the Atlantic break unswervingly against the mighty rocks which the Romans named Belerion or 'place of storms'. The tip of the British mainland is today dominated by a popular theme park covering Cornwall's history. Those preferring to get off the beaten track can instead explore the surrounding cliff and moor landscape on foot. The coast here boasts some spectacular scenery, with buffeted cliffs soaring up to 50 m (164 ft) out of the water.

Land's End is a symbolic place: It is the western end of the British mainland, and, in theory, the view from the edge of the cliffs stretches out to America. It can be reached from Sennen Cove via a delightful 30-minute hike along the Coast Path.

LAND'S END

ISLES OF SCILLY

The 140 Scilly Isles, accessed by ferry from Penzance, are located 40 km (25 miles) off the coast in the southwest. The approximately 2,000 local residents, who live predominantly off tourism and flower exports, are spread over five inhabited islands. While fishing used to be the main industry here, now it is tourism. With their rugged granite cliffs, white sandy beaches and turquoise bays, the islands are best explored on foot or by bike. Palms and exotic plants thrive in the mild climate, and a collection of typical Scilly flora can be found in the Tresco Abbey Garden. The English Atlantis, the lost country of Lyonesse mentioned in the Arthurian Legend, is said to lie halfway between Land's end and these islands, though it is yet to be found. There is, however, a series of wrecks to admire.

Hugh Town on St Mary's Island is the largest town in the Scilly Islands (left). The figurehead of the Thames steamship, which sank off the coast of the Isles of Scilly in 1841, today adorns Neptune's Staircase in the Tresco Abbey Garden (large picture). The Shell House (below, far left, top) in the same garden does full justice to its name, with an interior lined entirely with shells.

LONDON

London is a capital and city of royalty, the seat of the British government, an international financial hub, and a cosmopolitan metropolis in the truest sense. Until a few decades ago, London was the centre of the vast British Empire that spanned the globe and it retains a visible presence to this day.

The City of London – the historic town core – is a city within the city. It was originally the Roman Londinium, and continues to have its own administration. People have been trading and transacting money here for almost 1,000 years.

Capturing London in its entirety is no mean feat. There is the royal London with its palaces, the commercial London with its futuristic architecture, the historic London with its cathedrals and the 'old city', and the Thames, the city's lifeblood.

TOWER BRIDGE

Opened in 1894, Tower Bridge is not only one of London's leading landmarks, it is also a prominent example of the level of engineering that existed at the time. In the mid-19th century, London's East End was so densely populated that a bridge became necessary. Until then, all new bridges had been built west of London Bridge, so as not to impede the port facilities and shipping in the east. The solution was a combined bascule and suspension bridge. Steam engines activated the hydraulics system, which opened the bridge in the space of a few minutes. Today, this is done electrically. Both towers house exhibitions on the structure's history, while the now glassed-in pedestrian overpass high above the actual bridge provides sweeping views over London.

Spectacular by day or night: Tower Bridge acts as a monument symbolizing progress as the link between historic and modern London. A few technical details: The towers are 65 m (213 ft) high, the roadway (left) is 9 m (30 ft) above the river, and the pedestrian bridge 43 m (141 ft) above. The middle section is raised several times a day to allow tall ships to pass through.

TOWER OF LONDON

The mighty complex with the elaborate name of Her Majesty's Royal Palace and Fortress The Tower of London, but commonly known simply as Tower, stands guard by the Thames at the eastern end of the City. At its centre is the White Tower, a solid fortress building erected on the orders of William the Conqueror following his crowning as King of England in 1078. It was designed not only to protect the city against attacks, but also to enable the Norman rulers to keep a watchful eye on the independent and assertive Londoners. The two ramparts and moat were built in the 12th and 13th centuries. The Tower was a royal residence until well into the 17th century, a prison until the mid-20th century, and today remains a royal treasury where the Crown Jewels have been on display to the public for over 300 years.

ENTRY TO THE TRAITORS' GATE

The fortress by the river is visited by large numbers of people every year – not just for the grim tales of rolling heads and disagreeable noblemen starving in the dungeons, but also for the ancient ceremonies that continue to be held here for tourists, and the museum that provides information on the Royals. The Tower has been a UNESCO World Heritage site since 1988.

ST PAUL'S CATHEDRAL

The grand dome of St Paul's Cathedral rises proudly and distinctly amongst the City's office buildings. A Christian church has stood on Ludgate Hill here for 1400 years. The present-day English Baroque St Paul's is the fifth incarnation, and without doubt the most magnificent. The fire of 1666, which destroyed almost all of London, ripped right through the medieval St Paul's, and its reconstruction was entrusted to architect Sir Christopher Wren, who was also responsible for designing some fifty other churches in the ruined city. While Wren's plans were rejected a number of times, the foundations for the structure were finally laid in 1677, and the inaugural service was held there twenty years later. Christopher Wren was the first of many greats throughout British history to be buried here.

The elegant dome of London's finest religious building, modelled on St Peter's in Rome, is one of the city's main symbols and landmarks. With its high ceilings, sculptural decorations and rich ornamentation in the tremendous nave, it boasts a unique degree of baroque splendour considered rather atypical of the demure England of the time – prompting many contemporaries to deem the building too 'popish'.

BUCKINGHAM PALACE AND VICTORIA MONUMENT

Buckingham Palace is the official residence of the Royal Family, though only on working days and outside summer holidays. The palace therefore cannot be officially visited, except in the months of August and September, when nineteen of its rooms are open to the public. The magnificent residence essentially dates back to 1705, and originally belonged to the Duke of Buckingham. In 1837, Queen Victoria decided that St James's Palace no longer catered to her majestic needs, and moved to Buckingham Palace, which had been extended and modified into a veritable palace in the meantime. The most recent structural work was performed in 1913 to redesign the eastern façade, from whose balcony the Windsors graciously wave to the crowds below.

BUCKINGHAM PALACE AND VICTORIA MONUMENT

The Victoria Monument (left) was erected in the square opposite the palace's main façade in 1911. It is 25 m (82 ft) high and made out of 2,300 tonnes (2,530 tons) of white marble. The statue of Queen Victoria looks towards the Mall, and standing at the top is a statue of the goddess of victory. The monument's nautical theme is designed to commemorate England as a naval power. Below: Buckingham Palace.

THE ROYALS

The coronation of Elizabeth II in 1952 was the prelude to Eurovision in that it was the first major media event to be followed by millions of TV viewers for eleven whole hours right across Europe. Today, the British Royal Family continues to stir emotions, with the stories and scandals of its members fuelling the work of the tabloid press. While this does rock the notion of the Royals being a 'business', as they call themselves, the media never succeed in totally unhinging the House of Windsor. The Queen firmly follows protocol, but is increasingly making efforts to get closer to the people. For the last 40 years or so, for instance, a varying selection from the royal art collection has been put on display, and one section of Buckingham Palace is open to visitors during the summer months. Some of the Queen's dresses are also exhibited there. The strategy seems to have paid off, for these insights, among other things, prompted fashion magazine Vogue to name then-81-year-old Elizabeth among the 50 'most glamorous women in the world'. When asked themselves, the Brits say they would not want to lose their monarchy. The media interest these days is increasingly focused on the young Prince William and his brother Harry, from Prince Charles' marriage to Princess Diana, who died in a car crash in 1997.

Queen Elizabeth II has endured and lived through the highs and lows of the British Commonwealth, braving them with poise. She is pictured left with her husband Prince Philip, the Duke of Edinburgh. The wedding of Prince William and Catherine Middleton (large picture, right) in 2011 was a global media event. His brother Harry (middle), Philip and the Queen, here watching a flypast.

TRAFALGAR SQUARE

The entire history of the former British Empire appears to be concentrated at Trafalgar Square, which also reflects the nation's present in all its facets. Situated at the heart of the West End, the square was named after one of England's most important battles against Napoleon. It was near Trafalgar, southwestern Spain, that the British fleet defeated the armada of Spanish and French warships. The focal point of the square is the memorial column to Lord Nelson, who lost his life in said battle, while the bronze lions at the base of the monument are said to have been cast from the metal of the captured French cannons. Despite, or indeed because of, all this glory, however, the square also plays host to some of the most prominent demonstrations and largest parties, such as the New Year's Eve party.

The National Gallery, with its Neoclassical exterior, lines one end of the square (right), at whose centre stands the 51-m- (167-ft-) high Nelson's Column (below) – a popular meeting place for tourists.

PICCADILLY CIRCUS

Five busy streets, including Haymarket, Shaftesbury Avenue and Regent Street, all feed into Piccadilly Circus, prompting the vast square to be considered the gateway to London's West End and Soho entertainment districts and major shopping streets. It has always been a popular meeting point for tourists due to its central, easily accessed location on the heavily frequented Piccadilly Line. It is not, however, overly attractive, and is constantly crowded and noisy. Nevertheless, its reputation as the glittering centrepoint of London's nightlife remains firmly cemented. In 1923, giant neon billboards were added to every corner of the square, their lights flashing in the darkness promising endless options for consumers. Today, the billboards can only be found on one corner; traffic has now been reduced in parts of the square.

Unlike Piccadilly Circus, the street of the same name is more upscale, with the Ritz Hotel as its showpiece. It is also home to some truly regal shops, including the Fortnum & Mason department store, established in 1770.

WESTMINSTER PALACE

The neogothic exterior of Westminster Palace with its distinctive towers, including the Big Ben clock tower, gives the impression it has been reflected in the Thames since the Middle Ages. And the site had indeed been a royal residence since the 11th century. The present-day building, with the UNESCO World Heritage site of Westminster Abbey, was, however, not erected until the mid-19th century, after the predeces- sor structure was destroyed in a fire. the preserved sections from the Mid include the Jewel Tower and Westmin which is now only used for ceremonial The world's largest parliamentary buil its over 1,100 rooms, 100 staircases (2 miles) of hallways, is the seat of th government.

WESTMINSTER PALACE

A statue of Richard the Lionheart (large picture) guards the palace exterior. The Robing Room with throne (below, bottom) is where the queen dresses in the State Robe, before proceeding through the Royal Gallery (below, top) to open Parliament. The local landmarks here are at their most striking at sunset (left): the Westminster Bridge with Elizabeth Tower and Westminster Palace.

WESTMINSTER ABBEY

This abbey, officially the Collegiate Church of St Peter, is unique not only for its grand architecture, but particularly for its rich symbolism. With very few exceptions, all of England's monarchs since William the Conqueror have been crowned here – traditionally by the Archbishop of Canterbury –, and many are also buried here. The abbey similarly houses the tombs of other historic figures, including prominent writers, artists, scientists and politicians. Being buried in Westminster Abbey has always been the highest of honours. The structure itself is a mix of several different styles, as countless extensions and modifications have been added over the centuries. Nevertheless, it remains the finest example of English Gothic – and the most beautiful building in London.

While the nave of Westminster Abbey may be very narrow, measuring just 10 m (33 ft) in width, it is England's tallest, making it all the more grand. The design and interior today continue to serve as some of the most magnificent examples of medieval architecture, having been spared Henry VIII's dissolution and destruction of the abbeys. These days, Westminster Abbey is more of a museum than a place of worship.

LONDON EYE

The London Eye, a giant Ferris wheel situated between County Hall and the Southbank Centre, was officially opened by the prime minister at the time, Tony Blair, on New Year's Eve 1999, and has been one of the city's highlights ever since. Measuring 135 m (443 ft) in height, it is so far the largest Ferris wheel in Europe. When in operation, it spins continuously, but slowly, with a full rotation taking around thirty minutes. Passengers can board or disembark from the capsules without the wheel needing to stop. The thirty-two capsules are fully glassed-in and suspended on the outer ring of the wheel, giving passengers 360-degree views over London stretching for some 40 km (25 miles). The entire city is effectively at their feet. The London Eye was originally only designed to run for five years, but it was so popular that it is set to spin for another twenty.

The view is dizzying, not only because of its height, but also the impression it gives of the city's great size. Over fifty of the main attractions are clearly visible when the weather is pleasant. The London Eye is often compared to the Eiffel Tower in Paris or the Empire State Building in New York, as an equivalent symbol of the global metropolis of London.

LONDON PUBS

The traditional English pub is the heart and soul of the English nation; an institution that has shaped social scenes since time immemorial. It is where people go for drinks after work, where they exchange the latest gossip, where they meet friends, acquaintances and colleagues, and also meet new people. While this notion may have been watered down somewhat in a big city like London, the 'local' pub continues to play a major role – and is a great equalizer. Differences in class and age cease to exist; the pub is where generations and different stratas of society all come together. The public house, its official name from Victorian times, is an outdated affair. There is the bar with stools, a few tables and chairs or seating areas, wood panelling and carpet, usually a jangling slot machine, a darts board and, increasingly, a television. All orders and payments are made at the bar, with table service generally only provided when hot meals are served for lunch and – more and more commonly – dinner. The trend is gradually shifting towards the gastropub concept. Usually, however, the pub is a refuge for drinkers who traditionally enjoy an English ale.

The classic pint – just over half a litre – of ale or a cultured gin & tonic after a day of work or shopping is often enjoyed standing up in one of London's enchanting Victorian pubs. Most, such as the Royal Oak, The Shipwrights Arms or Sherlock Holmes (pictured below), have wood-panelled interiors and are affectionately decorated with souvenirs and all manner of paraphernalia.

THE SHARD

This eye-catching glass edifice soars to a height of 310 m (1,017 ft), and is the new landmark in Southwark. It was officially opened in July 2012, and the viewing platform opened to the public in February 2013. It has been a striking sight, visible from afar, ever since. The skyscraper even towers well above the London Eye, currently Europe's tallest Ferris wheel at 135 m (443 ft). The Shard sparked protests in its planning phase, with claims it would not fit with the rest of the city skyline. Problems with building permits, the sale of the land, and finally bailing investors led to delays in the project. Now, however, The Shard is a coveted attraction, with its seventy-two floors of residential units and office space, a luxury Shangri-La hotel, restaurants, bars, shops in the Shard Plaza, and access to the platforms of London Bridge train station.

As so often with major construction projects, the story of The Shard's creation is arduous and energy-sapping in parts, including all manner of controversies, but ultimately resulted in the city acquiring a new, popular attraction. Some 11,000 glass panes were used in the pyramidal exterior. Briefly holding the status of Europe's tallest building, it was eclipsed by Moscow's Mercury City Tower at the end of 2012.

NATIONAL GALLERY

Unlike most European galleries designed for the general public, the National Gallery at Trafalgar Square was established rather late. It is the only one of its kind not to have derived from any sort of royal collection. In 1824, the British government purchased thirty-eight paintings from the collection of deceased banker John Julius Angerstein, and displayed them in Angerstein's home on the Pall Mall. The new building at Trafalgar Square was finally opened in 1838 – as a place open to all sections of the population, not just the privileged art connoisseurs. Its halls constantly exhibit some 2,000 paintings from all European schools and eras, including some of the most prominent works by artists such as Vincent van Gogh, Claude Monet, Leonardo da Vinci, Paul Cézanne and Titian.

The National Gallery building was constructed in 1837. Lack of space prompted the addition of an east wing in 1872, and most recently the Sainsbury Wing in 1991. The Victorian building is an attraction in itself.

NATIONAL PORTRAIT GALLERY

Portraits of every famous Brit can be found hanging here, captured on canvas and enclosed in exquisite frames. Many can also be viewed in full size in the National Portrait Gallery, dressed in grand regalia or sitting on a chair. The gallery has been located at St Martin's Place since 1856, later moving to its present-day building directly adjacent to the National Gallery, where it has undergone two extensions over the years. One of the first pictures to be exhibited here was that of William Shakespeare, though photography also plays a major role. The collection contains around 250,000 original photos, the oldest of which date back to the 1840s. Old black-and-white photos of stars such as Vivien Leigh and Alec Guinness alternate with modern personalities such as the model Kate Moss or the Duchess of Cambridge, Kate Middleton.

The royal pictures, a veritable who's who of the British monarchy, are popular attractions at the National Portrait Gallery. Equally captivating are the portraits of figures from British history (right), including drawings, sculptures and even caricatures.

VICTORIA AND ALBERT MUSEUM

The sprawling building houses some 4.5 million objects of art, craft and design – from Europe, North America, Asia and North Africa, ranging from the earliest times 5,000 years ago to the present day. And as if that were not enough, the works encompass all creative forms, from sculptures, paintings, drawings and photos, to glass, porcelain, ceramics and furniture, to toys, clothing and jewellery. In short, it is the largest collection in the world. The museum was essentially built after the Great Exhibition of 1851, from which a few exhibits were purchased. It was originally intended to inspire design students as a manufactory museum. The number of exhibits grew rapidly, and more space was needed. As such, the foundations of the present-day building were laid in 1899.

The museum's façade and vast entrance area with its high dome (left) are a real feast for the eyes, providing the perfect setting for the lavish collection.

TATE BRITAIN

This museum houses a unique collection of British art from 1500 to the present. The new Clore Galleries building next to the Neoclassical main entrance is home to the estate of British romanticist William Turner. The prestigious Turner Prize, named after him, is awarded annually to younger British artists. Equally spectacular are the special exhibitions, which, in addition to being dedicated to individual artists, are often also designed as studies on various topics. Tate Britain was established in 1897 as the National Gallery of British Art or the Tate Gallery, named after millionaire Henry Tate, who, in the 19th century, had not only bequeathed his collection of contemporary art to the state, but also a sizeable amount of money to help build a suitable gallery for it.

The vast, wallpaper-like mural with fine gold-leaf work by British artist Richard Wright hung in the Tate Britain in 2009, earning itself the coveted Turner Prize. After the exhibition, Wright destroyed the piece as part of his performance.

EAST OF ENGLAND

The idyllic landscape of eastern England has long been attracting migrants from the Continent, with the Romans and Anglo-Saxons all leaving their traces here. Later, however, this region north of the Thames lost some of its prominence. To this day, it remains very focused on farming, characterized by villages, small farms, mills and pubs that provide the perfect setting to relax and unwind. Coupled with this are the vast, sandy beaches on England's driest coast, where there are often more seabirds than people, and an equally vast sky, whose cloud formations have captivated many a painter.

Sandringham House is of particular significance to the English royal family, who usually spend Christmas and New Year here. But it is also the place where Prince Charles met Diana.

SUTTON HOO

It's eastern England's very own Tutankhamun. In 1939, archaeologist Basil Brown discovered the unlooted ship burial site of an Anglo-Saxon ruler on the shores of the River Deben. It is reputed to be that of Rædwald of East Anglia, who died in the early 7th century. He was buried in a 27-m- (89-ft-) wide ship with exquisitely decorated weapons, trinkets and armaments, originating not only in England, but also Ireland, Scandinavia, the Merovingian Western Europe and the Mediterranean. While the ship and treasures did not withstand the passage of time as well as the burial objects of the Egyptian pharaoh, visitors to the Sutton Hoo Museum can see the king lying in state, just as he would have done on the day of his burial, through a life-size, walk-in reconstruction of the grave.

The Sutton Hoo Helmet (large picture), which is
one of many treasures on display at the museum
(below, top: the intricate details of a bag), is
covered in filigree detail work (below, bottom).
Left: The treasure of Sutton Hoo lay in the
middle of this Anglo-Saxon ship burial site. Iron
nails mark the position of the original planks,
whose wood did not survive the passage of time.

ELY

Ely Cathedral is also known as the 'Ship of the Fens', rising strikingly and majestically out of the surrounding Fens moorland. And it is to the Fens that Ely owes its prominence. When the Normans conquered Anglo-Saxon England in the 11th century, they were unable to capture the Isle of Ely, which was protected by the marshland. Only after William the Conqueror had guaranteed the city all its privileges did the residents surrender. In 1083, the small town, which still only has a population of about 20,000, was given a new abbey church, today classified as one of England's largest and grandest cathedrals. The 14th-century octagonal crossing tower is considered an architectural wonder. Its complex design features lavish partitioning in its interior, and draws eyes upward to the superb 43-m- (141-ft-) high star-like dome.

The cathedral's central nave (below, left) is just as impressive as the octagonal crossing tower (large picture and left). The Cathedral Church of The Holy and Undivided Trinity, as it is officially known, should ideally be visited when the sun is out – the unusual way the light streams in makes the stained glass windows look particularly bright, and the dome illuminated (left).

CAMBRIDGE

'Silicon Fen' is the nickname given to Cambridge, which has grown to become a hub for technology and science. Its university history dates back to 1220, when some scholars from Oxford migrated to Cambridge. The oldest college still preserved to this day, Peterhouse College, was founded in 1284, while the venerable St John's College has produced nine Nobel Prize winners. It was established in 1511 by Margaret Beaufort, the mother of King Henry VII. Its students have included writers such as William Wordsworth and Douglas Adams, as well as the co-founder of IT, Maurice Wilkes. Cambridge boasts a high concentration of historic buildings, and the grandest of all the colleges is King's College, established in 1441. Its chapel, completed in 1547, features a filigree fan-vaulted ceiling and magnificent glass windows.

The best known of Cambridge University's colleges is arguably King's College (below, right). Founded by King Henry VI, it is today the place where most courses are held. The chapel of the same name is considered a perfect example of gothic architecture in Perpendicular Style (below, left). Left: Greats such as Francis Bacon and Isaac Newton studied in Trinity College's Wren Library.

PETERBOROUGH

The city on the River Nene north of Cambridge is primarily known for its cathedral – one of the most original examples of Norman early gothic architecture. Unique in itself is the wide façade, with its three gables of equal height which rise up above giant arches. Once inside, visitors find themselves in a 147-m- (482-ft-) long and surprisingly narrow nave. The painted medieval wooden ceiling is the largest of only four to have been preserved across Europe. In stark contrast is the dizzyingly intricate 15th-century fan-vaulted ceiling in the chancel. Another tourist magnet just a few miles northwest of Peterborough is Burghley House, a stunning estate with parklands and an art collection. The city centre, the Iron Age Flag Fen open-air museum, the Nene Valley Railway Museum and Nene Park are also worth a visit.

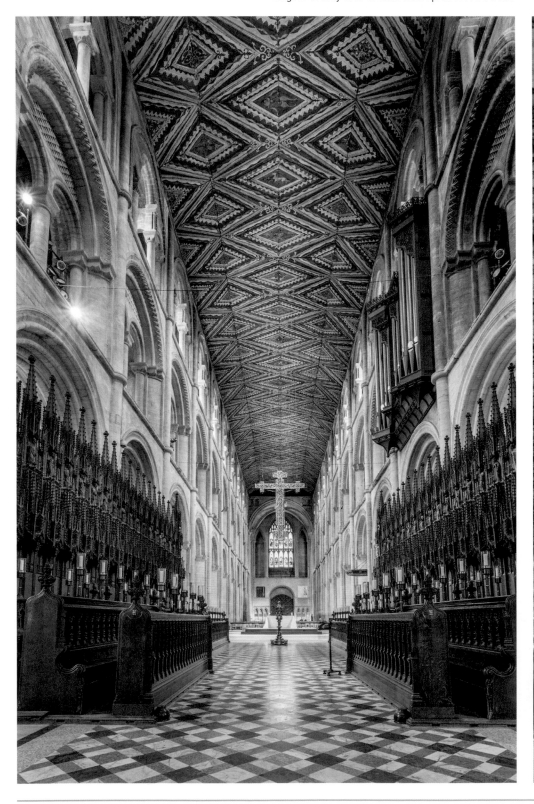

Left: The Butter Cross guildhall dates back to 1691. Far left: England is known for its stately manors, and one fine example of these is located some 15 km (9 miles) northwest of Peterborough. Burghley House is considered a masterpiece of the Tudor style. It was originally built on an E-shaped plan in honour of Queen Elizabeth I. Below and below, left: Peterborough Cathedral with wooden ceiling.

THE BROADS NATIONAL PARK

Like a completely different world, a 300 sq km (3,230 sq ft) landscape of rivers, canals and small, shallow lakes, which was created when peat was dug out back in the Middle Ages, stretches between Norwich and the coast. Numerous windmills attest to the efforts made to drain the marshes. Today the area attracts sailors and small motor boats, and increasingly also canoes, particularly on weekends and during the summer holidays. Hikes and bike rides in the Broads are other activities that can be enjoyed here. It was declared a national park in 1988 in a bid to protect the unique natural setting of this aquatic landscape, with its rare flora and many birds. Visitor centres exist in Hoveton, Ludham and the Whitlingham Country Park, while Wroxham is the main hub for boating tourism.

The soft light of the rising sun dances on the River Thurne and the Thurne windmill (right), one of many windmills in the area. Cruises on the River Yare (below) are also popular among holidaymakers.

NORFOLK COAST

The seemingly endless sky above Norfolk, with its ever-changing moods, provides a sense of calmness and relaxation for stressed city dwellers. The constant ebbing and flowing of the tides can be enjoyed on beach walks, while a stroll through the marshlands reveals many species of rare flora. And when it comes to seabirds, few other places in England offer a greater variety of birds or better opportunities for watching them. The end-to-end coastal walk boasts impressive diversity, be it trudging through the dunes at Holme-next-the-Sea, exploring vast marshland further east, or enjoying the view of the steep coast near Sheringham. What makes all this so beautiful is the fact that the landscape is not thrust into the foreground. The fresh breeze is instead the main protagonist here, providing perfect conditions for kite-flying.

The tricolour cliffs near Hunstanton particularly attract fossil hunters (below), while the little huts in Wells-next-the-Sea, a popular seaside resort on Norfolk's beaches, make for a romantic atmosphere (right).

NORFOLK COAST

EAST MIDLANDS

The eastern part of central England boasts a diverse landscape, with the lone summits of the Peak District in the west, the North Sea coast with its bustling seaside resorts and vast marshlands in the east, and the rolling hills of the Lincolnshire Wolds, with their ancient cultural landscape, in between. The East Midlands are among the earliest settlement areas in England, and cities like Lincoln and Leicester today still bear evidence of the important role they played as wealthy diocesan towns and centres of the wool trade in the Middle Ages.

Ancient volcanic rock shapes the landscape of Charnwood Forest, a densely wooded area in Leicestershire. It was also here that the first fossil of an approximately 500-million-year-old fern was discovered; the genus was named Charnia after the region.

LEICESTER

Right at the very heart of this bustling industrial city, which was founded in AD 50 as a Roman military camp, is a quaint Victorian centre bearing evidence of Leicester's long history. King Richard III, the hunchbacked villain from the War of the Roses, has been buried in the Norman cathedral since 2015. The skeleton of the king, who died in 1485, was found during excavations in Leicester in 2012. A museum now provides information on the latest research findings. Also worth a visit are the National Space Centre; the Abbey Pumping Station museum of science and technology; the Jewry Wall Museum, with findings from Roman times; and the New Walk Museum, with paintings from the German classical modernity movement, brought to Leicester by Jewish emigrants. The city is also known for its many Indian restaurants.

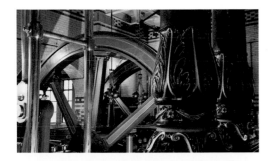

Leicester is packed full of technology and development, as evidenced by the Gimson steel engines at the Abbey Pumping Station museum (far left) and this space suit (left) at the National Space Centre. The centre is decorated in the lead-up to Christmas (large picture). And if it's too wet outside, you can instead shop till you drop at the Highcross Centre (below, top). Below, bottom: The town hall.

BELVOIR CASTLE

While the mighty complex on the edge of Belvoir Valley has the appearance of a medieval fairytale castle, it was actually built by James Wyatt, one of England's most famous architects at the time, for John Manners, the 5th duke of Rutland, in neo-gothic style in the early 19th century. The castle is still owned by the ducal family to this day, but is open to the public at certain times of year. Visitors can admire magnificent rooms more reminiscent of continental European palaces than an English manor, as well as an exquisite collection of paintings, including works by Dürer, Rubens and Poussin. The garden designs were created by English landscape architect Capability Brown, and the plans are finally being executed by the current duchess.

Visitors can explore the castle's lush garden on various Garden Walks, and encounter both exotic and local plants, including the stunning roses (below, bottom). Below, middle: Danish sculptor Caius Gabriel Cibber created six of the garden's statues. The castle also served as the set for the classic Christmas film *Little Lord Fauntleroy* (1980).

THE WASH

With a bit of luck, visitors can see seals here. In any case, England's largest population of small seals has chosen the sweeping bay known as The Wash as its home. Four rivers – the Great Ouse, Nene, Welland and Witham – mouth into the sea at this very point, located between Lincolnshire and East Anglia. They have deposited their sediments over the course of the centuries, constantly changing the bay's shape. Low tide, particularly at the shallow southern end, exposes sandbanks and endless mudflats, creating a paradise for redshanks, sandpipers and other coastal birds. In the hinterland, salt marshes alternate with swampy fens and farmland protected by dykes. Away from the seaside resorts, it is not long before visitors find themselves in a remote, secluded landscape, where they can enjoy the peace and a panoramic view virtually unobstructed by any hedges or buildings.

The marshland known as The Wash was flooded between the 17th and 19th century, and the landscape today, dotted with numerous waterways, is particularly popular among hikers and cyclists. Flora and fauna thrive here too. The section just outside Boston is heavily frequented by cockle-shell hunters (large picture). Grey seals are also occasionally spotted on the beach (below left, middle).

LINCOLN

Anyone visiting the capital of Lincolnshire needs to be light on their feet, for it was here that the Romans built their first military camp in Great Britain on a steep hill on the shores of the River Witham in AD 48. Steep Hill is worth the climb to this day, because the narrow, sharply inclining lane is lined with some of England's finest and oldest medieval buildings. These include the home of Jew Aaron of Lincoln and the adjacent Jews' Court, both dating back to the 12th century, when Lincoln was not only the richest city in England as a result of the wool trade, but also had a large Jewish community. Other must-sees are the High Bridge topped with half-timbered houses, the ruins of the Norman castle erected here on the orders of William the Conqueror, and of course the grand cathedral.

Lincoln Cathedral (below) is said to have been the tallest building in the world until 1549, because at that time, the mighty crossing tower had an extremely narrow, pointed pinnacle that soared 160 m (525 ft) into the sky. This spire was however not rebuilt after its collapse. Large picture: The High Bridge (or Glory Hole) from 1160. Left: The historic Bailgate district.

PEAK DISTRICT NATIONAL PARK

Surrounded by the industrial cities of Manchester, Sheffield and Stoke-on-Trent, the Peak District is England's oldest national park. Yet the city dwellers had to force their way into the countryside. It was only through an illegal mass trespass of Kinder Scout in 1932 that the private estate predominantly owned by the 9th Duke of Devonshire became accessible to the public. Hiking continues to be the most popular sport in the Peak District, though it is also a haven for cyclists, horse riders, climbers and paragliders. While the northern part around the 636-m- (2,087-ft-) high Kinder Scout – the Dark Peak – is dominated by vast heaths and raised bogs, remote peaks and spectacular rock formations – the White Peak – in the south present as a scenic hilly landscape of limestone plateaus, wooded valleys and small villages.

In just under three hours, hikers can follow a 5-km- (3-mile-) long trail up to the Mam Tor or Mother Hill. They are rewarded with one of the best and most breathtaking views of the national park. Below: The impressive Winnats Pass leads through steep limestone crevices. Far left: Crow Stones is the name given to these rock formations in the national park. Left: Losehill Pike.

WEST MIDLANDS

Industrial history can be truly fascinating! The region around Birmingham is not usually top priority on the itineraries of most travellers visiting England. Yet it offers an amazing array of interesting cities and buildings as well as diverse landscapes. It is here that Shakespeare was born, where the first ever cast-iron arched bridge spans the Severn, and where Coventry rose like a phoenix from the ashes after World War II. History has left its mark everywhere, and no other region is a more vivid example of fascinating innovations resulting from change and downfalls.

The Ironbridge Gorge near Birmingham is one of the places where the Industrial Revolution first began. The bridge across the River Severn was the first bridge in the world to be constructed from iron and is an impressive sight.

STRATFORD-UPON-AVON

Nowhere else on earth is William Shakespeare more venerated by his international fan base than in his hometown. Almost everything here appears to revolve around The Bard – from his medieval birth house, to the strangest souvenirs, to the modern Royal Shakespeare Theatre, where the best actors in the country can show off their skills. But this bustling small town would still be worth a visit even without its most famous son. The old half-timbered houses have been attractively spruced up, the beautiful parklands provide the perfect place to stop and relax, and cruises enable visitors to explore the picturesque River Avon. Or they can head to the Charlecote Park manor, where Sir Thomas Lucy is said to have once caught The Bard poaching and convicted him of the crime, prompting Shakespeare to immortalize him as a judge in *The Merry Wives of Windsor*.

Virtually everything in this city revolves around its most famous son, William Shakespeare. A procession of people in Elizabethan costumes is held every year, while at the theatre, the Royal Shakespeare Company exclusively performs Shakespearean dramas and comedies. But Stratford has much more to offer, including the Church of the Holy Trinity (below), the Old Bank (far left) and the Avon lock (left).

WILLIAM SHAKESPEARE – A TITAN OF LITERATURE

Shakespeare is an icon of Britain and the entire literary world. Many legends surround his life and works, due in no small part to the fact that none of them were preserved in manuscript form. Did he actually write all those world-renowned dramas and sonnets, or was it the nobleman Francis Bacon using a pseudonym? Some researchers believe the latter was behind historic dramas such as *King Lear*, comedies like *Much Ado About Nothing*, and even *Romeo and Juliet*, the ultimate romantic drama. Others surmise they may have been written by Christopher Marlowe. The only thing we know for sure is that, on 23 April 1564, a son named William was born to glovemaker John Shakespeare in the small town of Stratford-upon-Avon. Very little is known about his education or work until 1592, when he is mentioned as being a London-based actor and playwright. The following career path has been reconstructed for the years thereafter: member of famous troupes, performed for Queen Elizabeth I, became co-owner of the Globe Theatre, made friends with influential men, withdrew from the theatre scene around 1610, and returned to Stratford, where he died in 1616. His works had a global impact, and have even been immortalized by Hollywood.

WILLIAM SHAKESPEARE – A TITAN OF LITERATURE

William Shakespeare's literary works encompass some thirty-eight plays, numerous sonnets, and some verse narratives. His birth house (far left) is located on Henley Street in the half-timbered town of Stratford-upon-Avon, and he lies buried in the Church of the Holy Trinity (left). Large picture: a performance of *A Midsummer Night's Dream* at Shakespeare's Globe in London.

WARWICK

What happens when one of the largest castle complexes in England is taken over by the Tussauds Group? It becomes the most visited attraction in the country! Warwick Castle is today marketed as 'the greatest medieval experience' – with jousting tournaments, siege engines and re-enacted scenes from castle life. The outer courtyard is flanked by two towers – Caesar's Tower and Guy's Tower – and provides access to the medieval internal courtyard. The climb up the battlements is rewarded with a view over the Avon Valley. There is also a cabinet of wax figures, as is to be expected from Madame Tussaud's company, showcasing the life of the aristocracy in fully restored rooms. Those not prepared to pay the entry fees can head to the Avon Bridge to enjoy a view of the castle's exterior. The castle can hardly be seen from the city centre – which is incidentally also well worth a visit.

The Red Drawing Room of Warwick Castle (far left) is said to be haunted – or perhaps that is just a scary story told to the many visitors. It was fitted out by Robert Greville in the 17th century, and is named after the red walls on which hang two paintings from Peter Paul Rubens' workshop. Armour and weapons are displayed in the Great Hall (left).

COVENTRY

The name of this once beautiful half-timbered city is synonymous with the Coventry Blitz, the devastating firestorm triggered by air raids and fire bombs dropped by the German Luftwaffe on 14 November 1940 – a strategy to which many German old towns later also fell victim. But Coventry equally stands for the quest for reconciliation, with twenty-six partner cities and the symbolic Coventry Cross, whose nails come from the roof of the destroyed cathedral. The tall spire amongst the ruins was miraculously preserved, and had a unique new cathedral built around it in 1962. Coventry's history as an automotive city is recounted at the Transport Museum, opposite which is Millennium Square with the Whittle Arch – all of which are projects carried out as part of The Phoenix Initiative to make the city centre more attractive again. Incidentally, the phoenix has also been included in the city's coat of arms.

The gothic St Michael's Cathedral, built in the 14th century, was almost completely destroyed by bombs in World War II. Its imposing ruins today serve as a memorial (large picture). In 1962, architect Sir Basil Spence created the 'new' cathedral (left) alongside the old one. Below left: Whittle Arch (top) and the Glass Bridge (bottom) at the Transport Museum on Millennium Square are the work of MJP Architects.

BIRMINGHAM

England's second largest city has gone through a substantial transformation in recent decades. The centre which, with its smoking chimneys, was once the nucleus of the Industrial Revolution, is today a modern service-providing metropolis and lively melting pot of cultures. A large section of the population comes from the Indian subcontinent, the Caribbean and Ireland. In addition to historic Victorian splendour, Birmingham also offers premier shopping options and numerous theatres and art galleries. It also draws its charm from the many canals around Brindleyplace, which criss-cross the 'Brum', the nickname derived from the city's local name of 'Brummagem'. Riding one of the traditional narrowboats through the 60-km- (37-mile-) long canal system is an experience in itself.

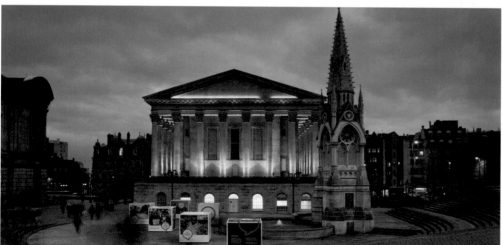

Birmingham boasts a fascinating mix of historic buildings and modern architecture. Large picture: The town hall with *The River* sculpture, also known as *Floozie in the Jacuzzi*, by the artist Dhruva Mistry. Below left, from the top: the Library of Birmingham, designed by the firm Mecanoo; Town Hall and Symphony Hall concert hall from 1834; and the Bullring shopping centre, designed by architectural firm Benoy.

SHROPSHIRE HILLS

The hills in southwest Shropshire today continue to be considered quiet and largely undiscovered, in stark contrast to the rest of the farming-centred region. The long-extinct volcano, in the form of the Long Mynd and its narrow valleys, rises up near Bishop's Castle, while the market town of Church Stretton, with its interesting Carding Mill Valley, nestles so picturesquely amongst the hills that it proudly bears the nickname of 'Little Swit-zerland'. The Stiperstones rock formations, created by weathering, are another striking sight, lining an 8-km- (5-mile-) long mountain ridge. An attractive hiking trail leads to Devil's Chair and Shepherd's Rock, perched at a height of 536 m (1,759 ft), providing a spectacular view of the mythical hill landscape.

Left: The Iron Age gave rise to a defence fortification on the iconic hill of Caer Caradoc, giving it its name to the hillfort. The originally volcanic peak rises steeply out of the otherwise flat landscape. Large picture: The green hills of the Batch Valley in the Long Mynd near Church Stretton. Below left, middle: The famous Stiperstones, which the devil himself is said to have scattered here.

STOKESAY CASTLE

Power relationships in the 13th century were known to shift rapidly, and wealthy wool trader Laurence of Ludlow wanted to fortify his new manor in Stokesay for this very reason, receiving official permission to do so from the king in 1291. And so it was that a complex with two towers and high outer walls was built around a central courtyard, though, from a military perspective, it would never achieve the status of a fort. The name Stoke-say Castle was not adopted into the vernacular for another 200 years. After the English Civil War, only the front ring of walls was demolished, making the complex today the best preserved of its kind. Interesting examples of medieval craftsmanship abound here, such as the original roof beams of the Great Hall. In the 17th century, these were joined by the amazing half-timbered gatehouse and the authentically finished private quarters.

STOKESAY CASTLE

Large picture: Stokesay Castle includes a gatehouse (pictured on the left) and two fortified towers (pictured on the right). Stokesay is a jewel of medieval fortified manors, and its Solar Room (far left) continues to display wonderful wood carvings on its walls. The room served as a private chamber to which the family would retreat after mealtimes.

IRONBRIDGE

Ironbridge Gorge with the town of Coalbrookdale in Telford, near Birmingham, is one of the pioneering sites of the industrial age, and a World Cultural Heritage site since 1986. Ironbridge Gorge owes its name to the bridge built here on the orders of iron-works owner Abraham Darby III in 1779. It is home to the 'Stonehenge of the Industrial Revolution': the first iron bridge in history, which spans the Severn Valley here near Coalbrookdale, and which can today still be used by pedestrians today. The nearby mines and coking plant are also open to the public, as are the railway installations that were built later on and enabled nationwide transportation. The well-preserved systems today form a vast museum landscape which vividly documents the start of the industrial age in England.

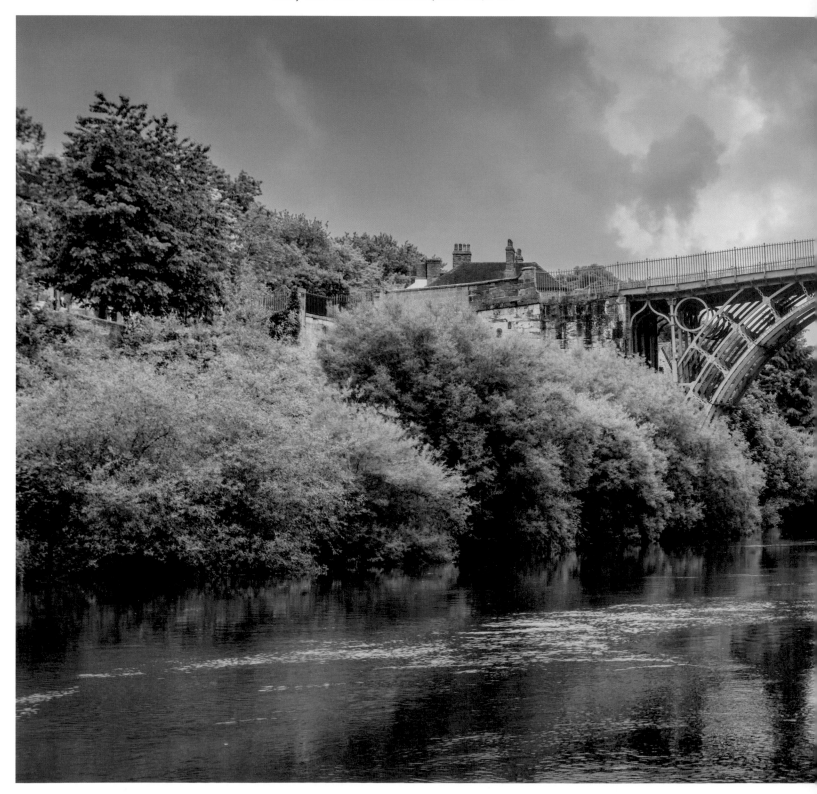

The Ironbridge complex, ranked as a World Cultural Heritage site, includes a furnace for iron-smelting, which was also built in the 18th century, the Blists Hill Victorian Town open-air museum and a brick-making workshop. The impressive bridge over the Severn (both pictures) is a gem of industrial heritage.

CHARLES DARWIN – FATHER OF THE MODERN THEORY OF EVOLUTIONS

Charles Robert Darwin (1809–82) is considered one of the most prominent naturalists of the 19th century. After completing his studies in theology, he undertook a five-year trip (1831–36) on the research ship *Beagle* at the recommendation of his botany professor Henslow. The trip took him past the islands of Cape Verde, around the east and west coast of South America to the Galapagos Islands, and onwards to Tahiti, New Zealand, Mauritius, Cape Town and St Helena. During the trip, the young researcher made observations and collected samples of rocks, plants and animals. Darwin would spend the rest of his life analysing his collections. This led to a wealth of new findings in the fields of geology, botany and entomology. But Darwin's most outstanding achievement was his modern theory of evolution, which explains the great variety between species based on the differ- ing development in characteristics, and accounts for the process of natural selection through differ- ent abilities to adapt to an environment. Darwin waited until 1858 to publish his revolutionary theory – the same year naturalist Alfred Russel Wallace published similar ideas. His groundbreaking work *On the Origin of Species* was released the year after, and *The Descent of Man*, and *Selection in Relation to Sex* in 1871.

Mammalia Pl

CHARLES DARWIN – FATHER OF THE MODERN THEORY OF EVOLUTION

It is not just the theory of evolution that is attributed to Charles Darwin. The British naturalist also explained the creation of reefs and atolls, recognized the role of earthworms in soil fertility, and wrote about carnivorous plants, the pollination of orchids, and the movements of plants. Large picture: Darwin's sketch of a vampire bat, created onboard *HMS Beagle*.

YORKSHIRE AND THE HUMBER

Windswept moors and heaths and wealthy industrial cities, secluded coastal trails and bustling seaside resorts, ancient culture and modern art: England's rugged north east between the mouth of the Humber and the Tees Valley is a land of contrasts. The time-honoured city of York, with its grand cathedral is just as captivating as the vibrant cultural scenes of the former industrial hubs of Leeds and Sheffield. Hikers will discover idyllic surroundings in the national parks, while the ruins of mighty abbeys and castles will have romantics swooning.

The hikers' haven of the Yorkshire Dales is located west of York, between the Lake District and the North York Moors.

LEEDS

A walk through downtown Leeds, with its many ornate Victorian buildings, today still reveals the wealth the textile industry brought to the city in the 19th century. But unlike many other former industrial cities, the capital of West Yorkshire managed the structural change very early on. Today, it is a university town and the centre of a metropolitan area, home to around three million people who are able to enjoy a cultural scene unrivalled by anywhere else in northern England. It includes the Leeds Art Gallery, the City Museum and the Henry Moore Institute, as well as some first-class stages. Industrial history is brought back to life at Armley Mills, which was once the world's largest wool-spinning mill. Coupled with this are excellent shopping facilities and a wide range of high-quality restaurants, pubs and cafés.

Left and below: The Briggate, one of the city's oldest streets, ran through Leeds as early as the 12th century. Today it is the main shopping street – pedestrianized and home to the Victoria Quarter with its many shopping arcades (below top). Large picture: Leeds' former Town Hall is an imposing sight.

YORKSHIRE DALES NATIONAL PARK

Anyone seeking solitude and views for virtually as far as the eye can see will love the Yorkshire Dales. The barren, hilly landscape of the Pennines, criss-crossed by river valleys, or dales, is characterized by sprawling pastures lined with ancient dry-stone walls. Climbing over these via one of the stiles or gates takes visitors into a rugged, karstic landscape of moors and heaths, with the odd wind-blown tree or bizarre rock formation protruding out in between. Most of the area is a protected national park. One of the best experiences to be had here is a hike along one of the many long-distance or circular footpaths in late summer, when the blossoming heather covers the hills in a deep purple. Among the more popular valleys is Wensleydale, home to the cheese of the same name, the ruins of Bolton Castle, and the television series *All Creatures Great and Small*.

The landscape of the Yorkshire Dales National Park is one of green hills, criss-crossed by the grey of the limestone, and occasionally a gnarled tree. Two valleys running in an east-west direction characterize the north of the national park, while the tourist-magnet valleys in the south stretch from north to south. Left: A red capercaillie peeps curiously out of the heather.

STUDLEY ROYAL PARK AND FOUNTAINS ABBEY

The Cistercian Fountains Abbey was founded by monks from York, and it ended up becoming one of the largest and wealthiest monasteries in the country through sheep farming and the wool trade. The 123-m- (404-ft-) long church, the 55-m- (180-ft-) high tower above the northern transept, and the adjacent monastery buildings have been largely preserved, albeit without a roof. The cloister, dormitory, refectory, 100-m- (328-ft-) long undercroft (storage cellar) and other storage rooms give an idea of the size of the complex. After King Henry VIII dissolved all the monasteries in England in the 16th century, the complex fell into disrepair, before becoming part of the Studley Royal Park in the 18th century. Created in 1727, the Georgian park with the Octagon Tower, Temple of Piety and Moon Pond is one of the most magnificent in the country.

STUDLEY ROYAL PARK AND FOUNTAINS ABBEY

Studley Royal Park in North Yorkshire is home to the imposing ruins of the former wealthy Cistercian abbey known as Fountains Abbey – one of the largest and best preserved monastery complexes in England, which has been a UNESCO World Heritage site since 1998. Fountain Abbey's nave continues to impress – despite its grassy floor and open-air ceiling (below).

YORK MINSTER

Measuring almost 160 m (525 ft) in length, York Minster is England's largest gothic church. Its sandy-coloured buttress rises up both majestically and elegantly above the red rooftops of the old town. Its interior is similarly brighter, and featuring higher ceilings, than most other medieval churches. The different gothic styles that were in fashion during its 250-year construction all combine to form one harmonious whole. The stained-glass windows play an important role here: York is home to the most, as well as the largest, medieval church windows in all of England. Those physically able to do so should definitely climb the 72-m- (236-ft-) high central tower, and enjoy the breathtaking views that unfold from there over much of Yorkshire – between elegant battlements and curious gargoyles.

York Minster was erected on the site of a Roman predecessor building. Construction of the 163-m- (535-ft-) long building began in 1220, and the completion of the western tower in 1472 gave the minster its present-day look. The magnificent structure is the largest gothic cathedral in Britain, and home to the bishop of York. Despite its size, the church still manages to appear light and airy thanks to its details.

NORTH WEST ENGLAND

England's North West is shaped by the Irish Sea. The ports played an important role here as early as Roman times, with overseas trade and the Industrial Revolution having an impact on the region later on. They brought great profit, and almost as many great problems, but also a constant wind of change that meant many new ideas took root here earlier than in other parts of England. Exciting cities like Manchester and Liverpool are joined by two of the country's most popular holiday regions: the Lake District and the coast with its seaside resorts.

The North Pier in Blackpool dates back to 1860. The seaside resort experienced its first boom in the mid-19th century, when many wealthy holidaymakers flocked here, soon to be joined by the working-class population of Lancashire.

CHESTER

Rightly considered one of the most beautiful cities in Great Britain, Chester is sometimes affectionately known as 'a slice of Elizabethan England in aspic', and anyone who strolls along The Rows, the famous two-level shopping arcades set amongst well-maintained half-timbered buildings, will quickly see why. Architecturally, the buildings feature a mix of Tudor and later Victorian design elements. And while not everything is original, this does not ruin the effect in any way. Today there remains no evidence of the fact that Chester was an important port in the Middle Ages. When the bed of the River Dee began increasingly silting up, the port lost prominence, and was superseded by Liverpool in the 18th century. These days, Chester lives off tourism, and is also world-famous for the cheese of the same name.

In keeping with its medieval look, Chester is home to an impressive gothic cathedral made from red sandstone (left). It was erected on the shrine to St Werburgh of Mercia, an Anglo-Saxon princess. As with the buildings in the inner city (below), however, it received a help in the 19th century, to maintain its medieval appearance.

SALFORD

Friedrich Engels once used Salford as an example to describe the squalid situation of the working class, and folksinger Ewan MacColl dedicated his 1949 song 'Dirty Old Town' to the city. With only a canal separating it from Manchester, Salford was one of the hotspots of the Industrial Revolution. The lasting legacies of this time include extensive port facilities known as the Quays, which began to fall into disrepair in the 1970s. In 1983, however, Salford became the first city to transform the industrial wasteland into a new, hip urban district. The construction of promenades, bridges and canals saw the system of paths and waterways adapted to the area's new purpose. Cinemas, restaurants, numerous outlet stores and water-sport facilities are popular with visitors. Spectacular stages and museums, as well as a fancy lift bridge, have all been created by reputable architects.

Salford Quays are primarily distinguished by their ultra-modern architecture – the work of renowned architects. The Lowry centre (below) comprising two theatres and art galleries was designed by Michael Wilford, the Imperial War Museum North (left) by none other than Daniel Libeskind, and the Lowry Bridge (far left) by the Carlos Fernández Casado engineering firm.

MANCHESTER

Manchester vies with Birmingham for the title of England's second most important city. While Birmingham is larger, the vibe in the metropolis of Manchester is more reminiscent of that found in cities like Barcelona. Nowhere else has the decline of traditional industry, with which Manchester was once synonymous, been overcome better than in this cultural and financial hub east of Liverpool. The Town Hall still attests to the city's former splendour, while The Lowry, the new cultural centre dedicated to the painter L.S. Lowry (1887–1976), sets a futuristic tone. The Manchester Art Gallery houses rich artwork treasures, and the Museum of Science and Industry provides information on industrial history. But it's not just art and culture that flourish here: the city is also symbolized by Manchester United, one of the greatest football clubs in the world.

The English have a soft spot for German-style Christmas markets, and here the lights of the stalls at the Albert Square Christmas market twinkle in the forecourt of the town hall (large picture). Other must-sees for visitors include the gothic cathedral (far left) and the opera house (left), where the European premiere of the musical *West Side Story* was held in 1958.

MANCHESTER FOOTBALL

There are few things people outside of England associate more with Manchester than its football. Headed by manager Alex Ferguson, and with celebrity players like David Beckham, Wayne Rooney, Cristiano Ronaldo, Eric Cantona, Gary Neville and Paul Scholes, Manchester United dominated European football in the 1990s and 2000s. While the club has now lost some of its shine – due in no small part to a sheikh's injection of cash into local rival Manchester City to boost competition –, ManU continues to be the highest-selling club with the largest fan base worldwide. It is impossible to imagine Manchester without football, and yet it was actually university students in Cambridge who discovered football in the mid-19th century and initially infected their classmates with the bug. Manchester United was founded in 1878 as a union of footballing railway workers in the district of Newton Heath, and Manchester City two years later as a parish team. But it was not until the 1950s that United, with its young team led by Bobby Charlton, began to dominate the English league. In 1968, ManU brought the European Cup back to the home of football for the first time, making Manchester synonymous with top-level football ever since.

Intra-city competition: things certainly heat up here in the matches between Manchester City (left: in league games against Bournemouth and Everton) and Manchester United (below: during the UEFA Europa League final against Ajax Amsterdam in May 2018, which Manchester United won 2:0 – two days after the city had been struck by a terrorist attack).

LIVERPOOL

Liverpool received its town charter as early as 1207, but remained a fishing village for 500 long years. Only when slave trading began was the first dock built in 1715, after which Liverpool played the most strategic role in the slave-trade triangle. It was here that weapons, alcohol and textiles were loaded and exchanged for slaves in West Africa, who were then taken to the Caribbean and America, where the ships were re-loaded with tobacco, cotton and sugar for transportation to Liverpool. Even after slavery was abolished in 1807, docks continued to be built – for purposes such as shipping emigrants, primarily to America. Liverpool experienced a significant boom following the arrival of immigrants from the Caribbean, China and, during the Great Famine of 1845 in Ireland. Six parts of the city centre and port were declared World Cultural Heritage sites in 2004.

With its impressive buildings and docks, Liverpool attests to Great Britain's rise to the rank of a world power. The docks were used until the mid-20th century, after which followed an economic downturn. The historic centre and docks were then reconstructed with EU financial aid. The five-storey warehouses today contain shops, bars, restaurants and museums.

LIVERPOOL AND BRITISH MUSIC: THE BEATLES AND MORE

Liverpool is where it all started. It was here that the G.I.s arrived for their D-Day mission during World War II, and they had more than just chewing gum in their bags. They also brought their music with them. The new rhythms and sounds found fertile ground in Liverpool. And then the city produced something entirely new with The Beatles: the birth of British pop music. From 1962 to 1970, the Fab Four were defining characters for pop and rock music, continuously exploring new realms of musicality. English bands dominated the evolving trend. The Rolling Stones, The Kinks, The Who, and all-round artists and singers like Elton John and David Bowie shaped the music tastes of young people all over the Western World. The songs created by these musicians consistently topped the charts worldwide. And the punk movement, originally intended as an aggressive form of protest against the commercially established pop culture, also has its roots here. The Sex Pistols and The Clash indeed soon started setting trends themselves. Newer developments similarly originated in England, and Britpop today remains a highly successful export, thanks largely to the pioneering work of the Beatles. In recognition of his services, former Beatle Paul McCartney was knighted in 1997, and Liverpool is now a UNESCO City of Music.

LIVERPOOL AND BRITISH MUSIC: THE BEATLES AND MORE

Liverpool honours one of its great sons – the bust of John Lennon, who was murdered in New York in 1980, can be found on the Wall of Fame on Mathew Street. Left: The Cavern Club, where the Beatles first performed live. Large picture: The Beatles – Paul McCartney, Ringo Starr, John Lennon and George Harrison – in 1967, after completing their hit album *Sgt. Pepper's Lonely Hearts Club Band.*

BLACKPOOL

LANCASTER

BLACKPOOL

Blackpool is England's largest seaside resort, and the epitome of British recreational bathing. Worker associations in the surrounding industrial cities began organizing excursions for their members as early as the mid-19th century. Where other seaside resorts have one pier with shops and amusement arcades, Blackpool has three. The amusement park is one of the largest anywhere, with ten rollercoasters, and the vast and opulent Victorian stages offer a dazzling array of musicals, vaudeville shows, cabaret, plays and concerts. The world's largest magic festival is held here in February, while the oldest and largest competitive dancing festival is staged in May and the Blackpool Illuminations bring night-time colour to the town in late summer. And there are of course beautiful beaches too. The water quality is good (once more), and North Beach is indeed even a haven of rest and relaxation.

With its giant Ferris wheel, Blackpool Central Pier is a great place to spend some time out (far left). The city's main landmark is the 158-m- (518-ft-) high Blackpool Tower, whose magnificent ballroom from 1894 still plays host to dancing events today (left).

LANCASTER

A climb up the Ashton Memorial is rewarded with the finest view of Lancaster and the sweeping Morecambe Bay. This 50-m- (164-ft-) high neo-baroque temple was built by a millionaire industrialist in memory of his second wife. He opened the surrounding parklands to the public as a gift. At the foot of the memorial is a university town filled with historic buildings, because Lancaster's location on the River Lune made it a prominent base even in Roman times. In the late Middle Ages, the marriage between heiress Blanche of Lancaster and Prince John of Gaunt saw it become the seat of the House of Lancaster, which waged the War of Roses with its rivals from York. In addition to the castle and medieval abbey church, the city's other attractions include the 18th-century port facilities and Maritime Museum.

The Edwardian Town Hall can today be hired for events such as weddings (far left). The Ashton Memorial above Lancaster makes for a scenic excursion (left).

TRACES OF THE CELTS IN CUMBRIA

As the famous English nursery rhyme goes, 'Old King Cole was a merry old soul'. According to a medieval Welsh source, King Cole (or Coel) is said to have ruled Hen Ogledd, the old north, following the Romans' retreat in the 5th century. Whether or not such a person did in fact exist is just as questionable as the existence of the legendary King Arthur. What is for sure, however, is that, after the Romans' military retreat, several Celtic principalities with a Romanized, largely Christian, upper class, stayed behind. They may even have brought Saxons, Angles and Jutes to the country as mercenaries to resist the invasions by the Scottish Picts, but they soon fell victim to the Anglo-Saxon invasion themselves. The Celtic kingdoms in the north, however, were still able to offer resistance for some time. Welsh epics particularly glorify King Urien of Rheged, who is likely to have resided in the present-day area of Carlisle, and even appears in the Arthurian Legend as a great warlord. He is said to have been murdered by a rival, prompting Oswiu of Northumbria, king of the Angles, to take over Cumbria in the early 7th century. The Cumbrian language died out in the 12th century, apart from the shepherds, who are reported to have still been counting their animals in Cumbrian – yan, yan, yhetera, methera, pimp – into the 20th century.

Mysterious traces of the past are scattered all over Cumbria, including the Castlerigg Stone Circle from the Bronze Age (large picture). Left: the ruins of a fortress from the Iron Age atop Carrock Fell in the Lake District. Below: Celtic crosses in cemeteries in Caldbeck, Irton, Kendal and Coniston (clockwise from top left).

LAKE DISTRICT NATIONAL PARK

The impressive landscape of mountains and lakes was made famous by 'Lake Poets' such as William Wordsworth in the 18th and 19th centuries. Spanning some 2,300 sq km (888 sq miles), and usually known simply as The Lakes, the area stretches for around 130 km (81 miles) northwest of Manchester. Several ice ages, particularly the Last Glacial Period that ended about 15,000 years ago, produced trough valleys with numerous lakes, and it is these that gave the national park its name. The Cumbrian Mountains make up much of the landscape. The upper regions are home to many cirques with ponds, while the lower areas are dominated by sprawling raised bogs covered in bracken and heather. Romanticist artists had been inspired by the scenery here right from the 18th century, dedicating their paintings and writings to the beautiful surroundings.

One of the most popular holiday destinations in England is the Lake District, which has been classified as a national park since 1951. The romanticist 'Lake Poets' repeatedly sang the praises of this landscape some 200 years ago, and anyone wanting to hike, climb, sail, windsurf or simply enjoy the scenery will feel right at home in this region of many lakes.

NORTH EAST ENGLAND

Those who enjoy secluded walks will feel at home in England's northeast. There are no bustling seaside resorts, and the miles-long beaches are often deserted. Mother Nature can also be admired at her purest along Hadrian's Wall in the North Pennines or in Northumberland National Park. At the same time, imposing castles and old monasteries attest to the turbulent history of this border region. Contrasting with all these idyllic scenes are the twin cities of Newcastle and Gateshead, which attract visitors with their state-of-the-art architecture, vibrant cultural calendar and pumping nightlife.

Lindisfarne off the coast of Northumberland is also known as Holy Island due to its monastery – the first English abbey to fall victim to the invading Vikings.

BARNARD CASTLE

While the small town on the Tees is named after its castle, it is dominated by the Bowes Museum. What looks like a gigantic manor in the style of a French château was designed by John Bowes in the late 19th century as a new home for his art collection, which the heir of ultra-rich coalmine owners wanted to make accessible to the public. Today, the Bowes Museum is considered the most eminent art gallery outside London, also display-ing a wide range of arts and crafts pbjects, historic costumes, furniture and fully furnished rooms. Another must-see are the romantic ruins of the actual Barnard Castle on the riverbank, immortal-ized by the likes of Charles Dickens in his novel *Nicholas Nickleby* (1839).

The Bowes Museum in Barnard Castle (large picture) holds a major collection of European paintings, textiles, ceramics and clocks.
Below: the staircase and drawing rooms in the Bowes Museum with original furnishings.
Far left: the ruins of Barnard Castle, which gave the town its name. Left: The eastern window of Egglestone Abbey (12th century) at Barnard Castle remains well preserved.

NORTH PENNINES

The northern foothills of the Pennines are England's third-largest nature reserve, and also the country's first geopark, due to their interesting and often exposed layers of rock. They are a haven for all outdoor enthusiasts – not just hikers, cyclists, anglers or bird-watchers. Special facilities are also available for horse-riders, climbers, kayakers, sailors, survival experts, cavers, geologists, biologists, stargazers and even skiers. Towering over the entire scene are the highest peaks of the Pennines: Cross Fell, Great Dun Fell and Little Dun Fell. Despite not even reaching heights of 900 m (2953 ft), they are covered in rare alpine vegetation, frequently shrouded in clouds, or buffeted by strong local winds. Anyone climbing them in fair weather, however, will be rewarded with a view extending as far as the Solway Firth and Scotland.

Red grouse and black grouse (pictured left) live in the heath landscapes of the North Pennines. Red grouse are hunted in late summer. On 12 August, the 'Glorious Twelfth', paying hunters from all over the world travel to northern England and Scotland to declare open season on them – a controversial and questionable pastime given the decline in grouse populations.

DURHAM

The Norman castle and three-storey Anglo-Norman cathedral in the city of Durham in the county of the same name in north-east England are examples of Norman architecture and the power of the bishops. They have been UNESCO World Cultural Heritage sites since 1986. Towering over the River Wear are the fort-like complexes of the bishops of Durham. A castle was built here in 1072; it was intended to serve as a bastion against the Scots, and ulti- mately became the centre of a Benedictine mon- astery settlement and a residence for the bishops, who were also the secular rulers of the region until 1536. Construction on the cathedral began in 1093 with a view to it housing the relics of the Venerable Bede and St Cuthbert. The church is considered one of the first structures erected by the Normans during the transition from Roman- esque to gothic styles.

Durham Cathedral (both pictures) is one of England's most prominent churches in Norman-Romanesque/early gothic style. As impressive then as it is now, it sits perched atop a hill along the River Wear. The ribbed vault above the choir is the oldest of its kind to still be preserved today, securing the cathedral an important place in architectural history.

NEWCASTLE UPON TYNE

During Roman times, it was here at Hadrian's Wall that civilization ended. For many people from the South of England, Newcastle upon Tyne is still a rough place, though the former 'Cinderella' on the Tyne has spruced itself up considerably. The façades of grand old buildings, blackened from a long industrial history, have been cleaned, the quays transformed into modern, vibrant urban districts, and striking new buildings erected. But in fact, Newcastle's biggest drawcard is its rich cultural scene. Anyone who comes to the city should not only visit its museums, but also explore its music and drama venues. And its dizzying mix of nightlife, with its many bars, pubs, clubs and restaurants from all corners of the globe, is considered the most exciting in Britain outside of London.

Grey's Monument (large picture) in the inner city is a popular meeting place. It is dedicated to Charles Grey, the 2nd Earl Grey (1765–1845), a British prime minister who is today mostly associated with the tea of the same name. Far left: St Nicholas' Church; left: Central Arcade. Below, top: the Northern Goldsmiths jeweller's shop; below bottom: the Tyne Bridge, opened in 1928 after three years of construction.

GATESHEAD

The twin city on the other side of the Tyne, Gateshead is connected to Newcastle by ten bridges. The most spectacular of these is the Millennium Bridge, whose semi-circular tread section lifts diagonally whenever larger ships need to pass through. But this city, whose centre fell victim to a devastating two-day fire in 1854, also boasts ultra-modern architecture. The Sage events centre, which stands on the shores of the River Tyne like a chunky, silver caterpillar, was designed by star architect Sir Norman Foster, and is considered the showpiece of computer-generated blob architecture (also known as blobitecture). With some 330 shops and an amusement park, the MetroCentre is the largest shopping centre in Europe, and standing above the city is Europe's tallest statue, the crimson *Angel of the North* designed by Antony Gormley, with a wing span of more than 50 m (164 ft).

Architectural milestones: The highlights of the old industrial cities of Newcastle-upon-Tyne and Gateshead include their bridges, such as the Gateshead Millennium Bridge, designed in 2002 by Wilkinson Eyre Architects (below). The futuristic concert hall known as The Sage, with its domed roof design, is the work of Foster + Partners and Arup Acoustics (left).

HADRIAN'S WALL

In a bid to better protect the Roman Empire against the peoples in the north, border fortifications were erected in the 2nd century, stretching across Europe for more than 5,000 km (3,107 miles). Hadrian's Wall runs from Newcastle, to Carlisle near the English-Scottish border, to Bowness-on-Solway 120 km (75 miles) away on the Irish Sea. It is part stone wall, part earth wall. Emperor Hadrian had ordered the construction of the 5-m- (16-ft-) high and almost 3-m- (10-ft-) wide wall in the years AD 122–132 to protect the people against the Scottish tribes. The fortification included the actual wall, built along a military road, as well as a military camp, smaller ('mile-castles') and larger castles, towers and gates. A moat ran along both sides of the wall. After the Romans' retreat around 410, however, the wall fell visibly into disrepair.

HADRIAN'S WALL

Hadrian's Wall, erected largely as a stone wall, was the Romans' attempt at protecting against the Scottish tribes. It and the Antonine Wall are part of the transnational Frontiers of the Roman Empire Word Heritage site, which also includes the German Limes line. Below: Milecastle 39 with Crag Lough Highshield Crags and Hotbank Crags. Hadrian's Wall is particularly well preserved at Greenhead (left).

NORTHUMBERLAND NATIONAL PARK

The area north of Hadrian's Wall was once a dangerous place; today, it provides an idyllic antidote to everyday stresses. Northumberland National Park, located between the wall and the Scottish border, is one of England's most remote regions. Hikers, nature-watchers and mountain-bikers all have ample room to themselves here. Yet there are also constant reminders of the many frontier battles waged here in bygone times. At the centre of the park is the Kielder Water reservoir, and hikers will be surprised by the large, open art installations along the 44-km- (27-mile-) long Lakeside Way. There are also observatories, for the national park is equally popular among astronomers. Here, far away from any cities and other artificial light sources, the dark sky is filled with thousands of twinkling stars.

Large picture: This tree is probably the most photographed tree in Northumberland National Park. It was made particularly famous by the film *Robin Hood: Prince of Thieves* (1991) starring Kevin Costner, and it was named 'Tree of the Year' by the Woodland Trust in 2016. The 'Robin Hood Tree' grows in Sycamore Gap, a dramatic dip in the landscape formed by meltwater near Hadrian's Wall.

LINDISFARNE

The name Lindisfarne is synonymous with tragedy. On 8 June 793, this little island off the coast of Northumberland was attacked by Vikings, who killed or abducted all its inhabitants. The attack is considered the start of the Viking age that sent Europe into a state of fear and terror for more than 200 years. It also resulted in the destruction of the monastery founded by St Aidan, and which had been famed for the Lindisfarne Gospels, a superb illuminated manuscript. The picturesque monastery ruins open to the public on the island today, however, date back to the 11th century, while the castle perched atop a conical hill was built on the orders of King Henry VIII following the monastery's dissolution. Anyone wanting to visit the 'Holy Island' needs to be mindful of the tides: at high tide, the sandy track that runs for some 5 km (3 miles) from the mainland to the island becomes submerged.

Below: The castle on Lindisfarne is nowhere near as old as the monastery. Located in the contested border region between England and Scotland, Lindisfarne Castle was built in the 16th century, just after the monastery (left) had been dissolved. The monastery's most famous abbot was Cuthbert, who tried to mediate during the Irish and Catholic conflicts of the 8th century.

WALES

As the smallest country in the United Kingdom, Wales has managed to preserve its cultural independence to this day. Celtic traditions remain alive and well – in terms of the Welsh language, festivals and customs. And yet there are equally clear signs of English rule. After conquering the province of Gwynedd in the 13th century, King Edward I ordered that a series of mighty fortresses – the so-called Iron Ring – be built there, and these have been listed as a UNESCO World Cultural Heritage site since 1986.

The Welsh Dragon is the symbol of Wales, and has also featured on its national flag since 1807. The dragon's origins are not totally clear, though it did appear as a Celtic symbol in the *Historia Brittonum* as early as the 9th century.

AND RAILWAY

TINTERN ABBEY

Tintern Abbey was founded as the first Cistercian monastery in Wales in 1131. Created out of the Benedictine Order by virtue of reforms, the Cistercian Order was one of the most influential in Europe in the 12th and 13th centuries. The abbey was redesigned in the second half of the 13th century, and the present-day ruins date back to that time. Monastic life came to an end in 1536 following the founding of the Church of England by Henry VIII; anything of value found its way into the royal treasuries. The buildings were conveyed to the Earl of Worcester, who immediately stripped the lead from the roofs and sold it, thereby initiating the abbey's decline. Ruins came into vogue in the 18th century, with many people making pilgrimages to the crumbling, ivy-covered walls. Artists and poets such as the romanticist William Wordsworth all drew inspiration for their work from here.

The Wye Valley, named after the river marking the border between England and Wales, was very popular among romanticists for its picturesque landscapes. This area in southeastern Wales is also home to Tintern Abbey, whose ruins have captivated numerous artists, including William Turner (1775–1851). Below: View westwards through the nave of the former abbey.

CARDIFF

Cardiff, the largest city in Wales, has also been its capital since 1955. The town was still small and insignificant at the start of the 19th century, before industrialization saw it experience a rapid boom. The port became an important transshipment site for what was considered the fuel of progress at the time: coal. Following the decline of heavy industry, Cardiff evolved into a centre of science and culture, with a university and prominent thea- tre and opera house. Another famous site is the Red Castle, Castell Coch, in Cardiff's north – an opulent, neogothic-inspired building from the 1870s. The flipside of the region – the steel works and coal mines, the abandoned sites of the Indus- trial Revolution – can be visited at the UNESCO World Heritage site in Blaenavon north of Cardiff.

Large picture: The imposing Wales Millennium Centre (designed by Jonathan Adams) with its two stages is one of the city's main landmarks. Below left, top: Cardiff Castle today consists of a medieval castle and a fairytale neogothic manor in Victorian style. Below left, bottom: The Welsh Parliament, known as The Senedd and designed by Richard Rogers, stands right by the sea.

WELSH TRADITIONS

National dresses help build an identity – and Lady Llanover (1802–1896) may have shared this line of thinking when she propagated her ideas about authentic Welsh dress. But she may also have had an eye on the local wool industry. In any case, she was successful, because the combination of a black hat with lace hem, a lace collar, a pinafore and a scarf today continues to be considered the 'authentic Welsh women's costume'. While experts claim the smart combination is a product of the 19th century, fusing various influences, this does nothing to break the Welsh spirit. The tradition of the Morris Dance is not genuinely Welsh either. This type of folkdance has managed to be preserved right across the Anglo-Saxon world, prompting people to now deem it an authentically English (or Welsh) particularity. No one can agree on the origins of this dance form, but there is considerable evidence to suggest that it has something to do with the Moors' expulsion from Spain (1492), and that the 'Moorish dance' became the 'Morris Dance'. The folkdance was originally only performed by men, though women are now also allowed to participate. Dancers in Wales often like to wear the national colours of red, white and green when doing so.

Below: The name of the Welsh custom Mari Lwyd means 'grey mare' in English. On New Year's Eve, small groups of people in the South of Wales go wassailing from house to house with a 'mare' and sing songs to beg for food. Left: The Langollen Eisteddfod cultural festival and Welsh national dress.

CAERPHILLY CASTLE

The castle north of Cardiff dates back to Gilbert de Clare, one of the most powerful men under Henry III and Edward I. Between 1268 and 1280, he ordered the construction of a mighty complex to protect the southern flatlands against the Welsh princes from the mountainous regions. Throughout the entire United Kingdom, only Windsor Castle is larger. The initial design was for a concentric castle with two curtain walls, protected by two artificial lakes. This basic idea then served as the blueprint for all castles built under Edward I in northern Wales. But Caerphilly Castle soon lost its importance and fell into disrepair. The corner towers still intact were demolished in 1649. It is thanks to the wealthy marquesses of Bute that much of the castle was carefully restored, starting in 1870. Only since the re-damming of the lakes has Caerphilly Castle begun to regain its former imposing appearance.

Caerphilly Castle is the largest castle in Wales, and the second largest in Great Britain after Windsor Castle. It has laid vacant since the 14th century, though legend has it that the Green Lady, the spirit of the former wife of Gilbert de Clare, can be spotted here during the full moon, roaming the castle's hallways dressed in green.

ST GOVAN'S CHAPEL

SOLVA

There are few places as atmospheric as St Govan's Chapel. The stone chapel, providing spectacular panoramic views over the sea, has been partly hewn out of the cliffs. It is only accessible via fifty-two descending stone steps, and is a rare gem in this barren region. The legend surrounding its construction states that the monk Govan lived in a cave nearby. When he eventually died, he was buried at the exact point where the altar stands at the eastern end. But many details today still remain unclear when it comes to the chapel. Some parts are said to date back to the 6th century, while the current building is likely to be from the 13th century. The limestone walls enclose a 5 by 4 m (16 x 13 ft) space. It is particularly worthwhile to check out up-to-date opening information before you go, for St Govan's Chapel should only be visited when the nearby shooting range is closed.

The tiny chapel is only accessible by via fifty-two steps that lead down from the cliffs.

SOLVA

Postcards of the fishing village of Solva (or Solfach) blow visitors away, because in one sense, the town appears to sit right on the water, and in another, it appears inland. Both are correct, and the reason for this is the tides. The narrow bay is usually completely dry at low tide, while at high tide, the water sloshes against the port walls. In the Middle Ages, lime-burning was one of the main sources of income here, and some of the furnaces have today still been preserved and are open to the public. In the 19th century, meanwhile, the focus shifted to maritime trading. At that time, thirty-one registered trading ships were docked at the town, which these days looks extremely picturesque. The many brightly painted little houses are particularly popular among tourists, who have long replaced the maritime trade as a source of income. Surfers and other watersport enthusiasts feel right at home in Solva – perhaps because of the attractive beach that lies just a few minutes' walk from the town.

Solva is arguably the prettiest fishing village in Pembrokeshire. The pubs and cafés at the port are perfect places to stop for a bite to eat.

ST DAVIDS

St Davids is the westernmost city in Wales, situated on the north coast of St Brides Bay. The reason the small town qualifies as a city is thanks to its cathedral – a church of such stature can only stand in a city, no matter how small the town's population. And it is not just any old cathedral; it is the largest in Wales. In the Middle Ages, it was an important centre for pilgrims; St David (circa 512–587), the patron saint, worked there as an abbot and missionary. The present-day church building dates back to the 12th century. Despite its gothic elements, the interior is essentially Norman. The carved wooden ceiling from the 16th century is an imposing sight, and the choir stalls and Bishop's Throne also display artistic carvings – including scenes from everyday farming life.

Below: A church has stood on this site for about 1500 years. While most of the present-day St David's Cathedral dates back to the 12th century, it has undergone numerous modifications over the years. Left: Apart from the cathedral, the city of St Davids boasts a pretty centre with luxury hotels and winding lanes perfect for leisurely strolls.

PEMBROKESHIRE COAST NATIONAL PARK

If you find yourself passing street signs with names like Fford Cilgwyn, Llwyngwair, Feidr Cefn or Gellifawr – unpronounceable to English speakers –, it means you are in the wondrous world of Pembrokeshire Coast National Park. And just as these names conjure up images of fairies and elves, so the landscape also creates the feel of a magical kingdom of nature. This is particularly the case along the snaking Pembrokeshire Coast Path, one of Great Britain's most breathtaking coastal hiking trails, where cliffs, bays and sandy beaches alternate in rapid succession. Fifty different species of flower, from hyacinths to plumose anemones start blooming here as early as January due to the mild climate. And this sea of colour later also becomes the breeding ground for thousands of seabirds, including puffins, oystercatchers, cormorants and razorbills.

Naturalist and author Ronald Lockley presented a plan for a route along the Welsh coast in 1953, and the Pembrokeshire Coast Path was opened in 1970. Usually split into fifteen stages, the extensive path runs for some 300 km (186 miles) virtually right along the top edge of the steep cliffs. The many bays provide spectacular views.

BRECON BEACONS NATIONAL PARK

It is not uncommon for hikers in the remote Brecon Beacons to suddenly find themselves face to face with a billy goat who refuses to move out of the way. He appears to size hikers up quizzically, and once he has won the power play, he magnanimously steps aside. That is when it becomes clear who the goat is. It is Merlin, of course – the Druid from King Arthur's Round Table, who is buried here in the south of Wales, and who occasionally appears to people as a goat. And given Merlin was also a mystic, it is no wonder he tends to roam around the mystical landscape of Brecon Beacons. The mountain range is the centrepiece of the national park that was founded in 1957. The hike along the 'horseshoe' of the four peaks of Pan y Fan, the highest mountain (886 m/2,907 ft) in the Brecon Beacons, takes around six hours from Storey Arms, the old stagecoach station.

The Brecon Beacons National Park is known for its mystical landscapes, particularly the Llangattock Escarpment – a series of bizarre limestone cliffs overlooking the Usk Valley (large picture). Below, middle: ruins of the 12th-century Carreg Cennen Castle; bottom: Waterfall Country is the name given to the southern section of the national park, home to the cascading Sgwd Ddwli Uchaf.

HAY-ON-WYE

Literature plays a major role in the book town of Hay-on-Wye. The Hay Festival of Literature & Arts held there annually since 1988, was once labelled the 'Woodstock of the mind' by former U.S. President Bill Clinton. Today, bibliophiles from all over the world meet in this small town at the northern tip of the Brecon Beacon National Park all year round. Many buildings are literally packed to the rafters with books. And there are some twenty-five second-hand bookshops, despite a population of not even 2,000. Hay-on-Wye has existed as a literary village since 1961, when bookseller Richard Booth opened his second-hand bookshop and spread the idea of the 'book town', attracting many more such stores. The town is also home to the ruins of Hay Castle, which today double as a marketplace for – what else but – used books.

The numerous second-hand bookshops and bookseller's stores in Hay-on-Wye, the world's largest book town, have more than just attractive first editions of poems by Welsh national poet Dylan Thomas on their shelves. Right: The town's Clock Tower.

POWIS CASTLE

A highlight on any trip to Wales is a visit to this unusual castle complex near the English border. The red sandstone of its towers and walls glows as it sits perched atop a mountain ridge above the world-famous gardens below. The blossoming terraces with their ancient arborvitae trees majestically cascade down to the manicured lawns and hedges and a small country park. The solid castle was first erected in 1200, and has constantly been modified for added comfort. It managed to escape destruction, and consequently boasts elements of all architectural styles until the 19th century. Henrietta Herbert, the daughter of then-Lord Powis, and her husband, Baron Edward Clive, were key figures associated with the castle. She was responsible for the gardens, while he, as Commander-in-Chief of British India, collected a number of treasures which are today exhibited in the museum.

The landscape gardeners of Powis Castle resisted the 18th-century trend of strictly formal designs, resulting in Powis today being one of the few complexes in Britain still displaying a purely baroque country garden.

POWIS CASTLE

ABERYSTWYTH

The university town of Aberystwyth is the administrative centre of the west coast of Wales. Known by its residents simply as 'Aber', the city stretches between three hills and two beaches. One of the hills, Pen Dinas, today still bears the ruins of an Iron Age fort, while on Constitution Hill, a café has been joined by a camera obscura showing the city and landscape as a projection, for the view from up here provides a spectacular panorama of the town and coast. The port, into which the rivers Ystwyth and Rheidol flow, once played a key role in trade with Ireland, and sometimes even in trans-Atlantic trade, though this is no longer the case. Penglais Hill is home to the National Library of Wales and the university, whose most famous former student is Prince Charles.

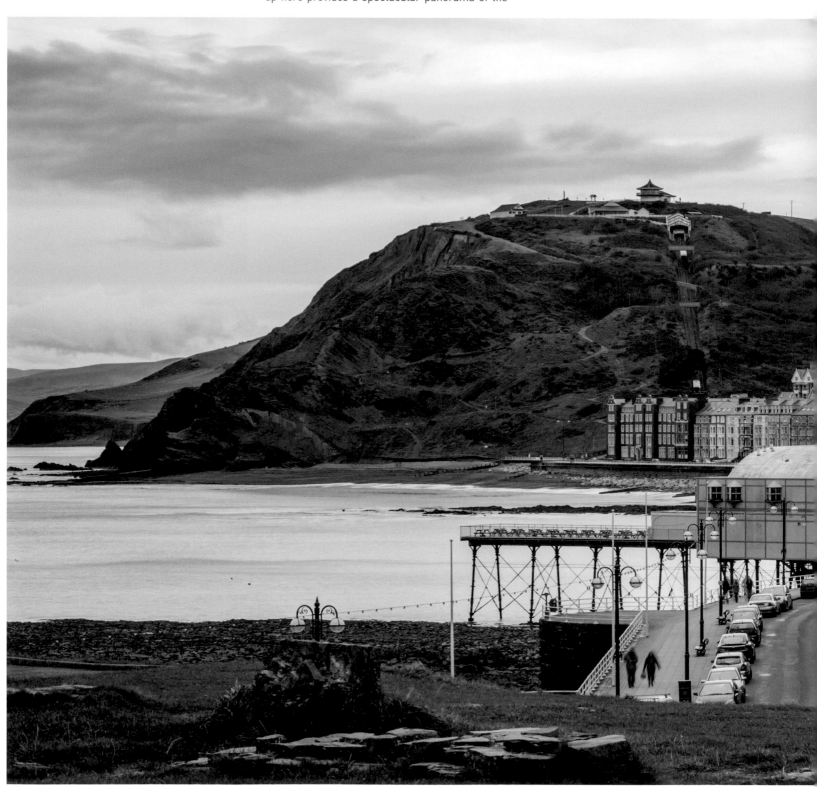

Left: The seaside promenade of Aberystwyth bathed in the glow of the setting sun. Below: Aberystwyth University, set before the 143-m- (469-ft-) high Constitution Hill, which provides views stretching as far as Snowdon on a clear day. A small mountain railway built in 1896, the Aberystwyth Cliff Railway chugs up the hill at a leisurely 6 km/h (4 mph). Passengers can enjoy a stop at the hilltop café after the ride.

HARLECH CASTLE

High above the golden sandy beaches, a fortress clings to the cliffs like an eagle's eyrie. Harlech Castle once guarded the port here at Tremadog Bay, which is widely considered the place where English troops led by Otto de Grandson landed in 1283. King Edward I spared no expense in ordering the rapid construction of a fortress system to fight the insurgent Welsh and re-integrate Wales into English territory. So it was that the medieval complex was completed in just six years, and has remained virtually unchanged to this day. Only the landscape has ceased to be the same. At the time, the lords would access the sea, which used to be right under the cliffs, via a staircase. But the coast increasingly silted up over the centuries, and the ocean is today more than 1 km (1,000 yds) away.

HARLECH CASTLE

Harlech Castle is part of the 'Iron Ring' of castles built under Edward I following the conquest of Wales. It played a key role in many historic events, including as a place of refuge for Margaret of Anjou during the Wars of the Roses, and numerous Welsh uprisings. Left: A backdrop featuring the 1,085-m- (3,560-ft-) high Snowdon, which is also accessible via narrow-gauge railway.

EDWARD I, CONQUEROR OF WALES

Edward (1239–1307) began demonstrating his fighting spirit right from his time as crown prince. The English royalty's main adversary was Simon de Montfort – leader of the rebelling English barons and ally of the Welsh Celtic prince Llewelyn ap Gruffydd. Prince Edward had in turn struck a deal with Welsh noblemen whom Llewelyn wanted to topple, and managed to annihilate the Montfort camp in 1265. This marked a temporary end to the battles, at least in England. Edward I was crowned king in 1274. Llewelyn's refusal to bow down to him prompted Edward and his army to invade Wales. All previous conquerors had steered clear of the wild peninsula. But Edward besieged Llewelyn in the Snowdon Massif and forced him to capitulate. It was only after a second campaign (1282–83), however, that the Welsh surrendered. To secure the new sovereign territory, the king ordered the construction of mighty fortresses in Gwynedd. And he appointed his son, the future King Edward II, as the prince of Wales. The English heir to the throne has borne the title of Prince of Wales ever since. Edward I was also known colloquially as the 'Hammer of the Scots' and 'Longshanks', because he not only had a mighty stature in terms of warfare, but also measured a stately 1.88 m (6 ft) in height.

Conwy Castle (large picture: painting by British artist William Daniell, 1769–1837) is part of the 'Iron Ring' of fortresses erected along the North Wales coast on the orders of Edward I (portraits left and below right). The castles are prominent examples of medieval military architecture, monuments of the small nation's colonization by the English Crown, and have been a World Cultural Heritage site since 1986.

PORTMEIRION

Some find it odd, others see it as genius. Regardless, everything here follows the illusion of an Italian village – as if Portmeirion were on the Mediterranean rather than a headland of the stormy Welsh coast. It was established as a holiday village of sorts in 1925 by eccentric architect Clough Williams-Ellis, who converted the handful of houses into accommodation. He spent fifty years working on this fantasy world, with many building elements coming from demolished buildings. Upon closer examination, almost everything turns out to be a colourful backdrop and considerably smaller in real life – a fascinating play of sight lines and optical illusions. The village stretches from the gatehouse to the cathedral and piazza, and down to the bay with its hotel and lighthouse. The surrounding parklands, on the other hand, are 100 per cent real, with enchanting pathways and great views.

Wales - or should that be Italy? Portmeirion could easily be mistaken for a Mediterranean coastal town. Created in Italian Mediterranean style by Sir Bertram Clough Williams-Ellis from 1925 to 1975, the hotel village particularly became known through the British television series *The Prisoner* (1967–68).

WELSH STEAM TRAINS

Grown men instantly become young boys again as soon as they hear the hissing and clattering of the traditional Welsh steam trains. The plumes of white, or sometimes jet-black, smoke, the smell of coal and axle grease, and the sight of the restored train slowly setting into motion sends them to Cloud 9. The fact that the abandoned narrow-gauge and traditional railways have been reconstructed and put back in operation is largely thanks to museum associations and volunteers. The Welsh Highland Railway from Porthmadog to Caernarfon was totally rebuilt, with work being completed in 2011. The narrow-gauge railways once transported shale and coal to the local centres and along the main tracks. The trains were small to keep costs low, and they look like toys by today's standards, but they are genuine powerhouses capable of effortlessly handling even steep climbs. The moun- tainous region of Snowdonia is home to the most breathtaking sections which lead all the way up to Snowdon itself. The Ffestiniog Railway from Porth- madog to the mountains is the oldest, and the steam trains from 1863 today once again operate along it. The Rheidol, Fairborne and Talyllyn Rail- ways head further south along the west coast, while the Brecon Mountain and Welshpool & Llanfair Railways also unlock areas of magnificent beauty.

Large picture: a steam train on the oldest route, the Ffestiniog Railway, pulling into Porthmadog. Left: Dafydd Lloyd George steam train at Tan-y-Bwlch station, also on the Ffestiniog Railway. Below, top: a Garratt steam train pulling into Porthmadog; bottom: a Corwen Revival steam train at Berwyn station on the Llangollen Heritage Line.

SNOWDONIA NATIONAL PARK

Once upon a time there was a giant named Rhudda, who lived on a mountain and wore a coat made from the beard hair of kings he had slain – until King Arthur killed him. Legend has it that, ever since, Rhudda has been resting on his mountain, which the Welsh thus call Yr Wyddfa or 'the tomb'. In English, it is known as Snowdon, and it is both the name-giver and highlight of the national park in northern Wales. Its mountain lakes are deep blue, and its slopes a ghostly green. Often, however, all colours are soaked up by the mist and clouds. The area gets more than 5 m (16 ft) of rainfall every year; the summers are hot, the winters are bitterly cold, and there is no shelter from the wind. Visitors to Snowdonia need to be on their guard, particularly against mountains like Cadair – because, according to legend, anyone who spends the night on it goes either blind or insane.

The legendary landscapes of the Snowdonia National Park can be explored on a variety of routes. Left: Mountain streams tumble through the wildly rugged rocky landscape. Far left: The Llyn Gwynant moraine lake is a popular destination for kayakers and canoeists. More than seven trails lead up to Snowdon's summit (below), but climbers need to be sure-footed and have a head for heights.

CAERNARFON CASTLE

Gwynedd is a rugged region in northern Wales which was governed by small noble families for centuries. Construction began on Caernarfon Castle at the mouth of the River Seiont on the orders of Edward I in 1283, once his troops had subordinated the previously independent Wales. Located around 13 km (8 miles) south of Bangor, the building, with its octagonal towers, is one of the most impressive castle complexes in Wales.

Not only was it designed to be part of the 'Iron Ring' of defence, the castle was also the king's residence and the seat of his government. It was there that, in 1284, Edward's eldest son, who later became King Edward II, the first Prince of Wales, was born. In 1969, this title was officially conferred upon the heir to the throne, Charles Mountbatten-Windsor (Prince Charles), at the castle.

Caernarfon Castle was intended to demonstrate power and command respect, and it is indeed architecturally one of the most impressive castles in Wales. Consisting of several portcullises and gates, plus – unlike other castles in Wales – octagonal towers and solid walls decorated with sandstone and limestone, the ruins are listed as a UNESCO World Cultural Heritage site.

ANGLESEY

ANGLESEY: BEAUMARIS CASTLE

In the northwest of Wales, near the Snowdonia mountain ridge, lies the island of Anglesey, connected to the mainland by two bridges. The fertile island was considered the breadbasket for northern Wales in the Middle Ages. It was once also a cult centre for the Druids, though the Romans destroyed the sanctuary and killed all the Druids in AD 61 as a way of crushing the resistance shown by the Celtic population. The island – particularly the pretty Llanddwyn peninsula – today continues to be attributed with magic powers, a notion aided by its megalith complexes. The island came to fame as being home to the town with the longest name in Europe: Llanfairpwllgwyngyllgogerychwyrndrobwllllantysiliogogogoch. The fifty-eight-letter monstrosity of a word is, however, usually abbreviated to Llanfairpwll or Llanfair PG.

The small medieval church stands on Anglesey's Llanddwyn peninsula (below). Just off the island's west coast is the tiny Holy Island, with its South Stack Lighthouse from 1809 (left).

ANGLESEY: BEAUMARIS CASTLE

Towers and walls dot the lush coastal landscape, painting a picturesque scene. After Edward I finally defeated the Welsh revolt, he wanted to ensure his rule was also cemented in Anglesey. The moated castle on Menai Strait, whose construction began in 1295, was his largest and last. And it was the only one of his castles never to be completed, because Edward needed the money for other conflicts in the meantime. With its perfect symmetry and ring-shaped outer bailey between the walls, however, it still exemplifies the influential role of English fortress architecture. Edward's intention was no doubt also for the nearby town of Llanfaes, northern Wales' centre of trade, to yield to the construction, and for an English port and administrative seat to be established under the castle's protection. The quaint Victorian town today still bears evidence of its former prominence.

Left: The view out towards Snowdonia National Park also includes Beaumaris Castle, another castle erected by Edward I, and considered one of the finest examples of 13th-century fortress construction.

CONWY CASTLE

Perched atop a rocky promontory, the mighty castle with its eight towers rises up above the Conwy River. It was Edward I's first and most important fortress in northern Wales. Construction began in 1283 and took just five years to complete under the direction of master builder James of Saint George. The centrepiece of the 'Iron Ring' is nothing more than a show of power, demonstrating the king's right to control Wales. With its two courtyards and royal apartments, however, it still had very comfortable amenities. No less impressive is the city wall built at the same time. It follows on directly from the castle, providing the English with a secure base in enemy territory. Unfortunately, the immense castle ruins today appear jammed between roadway and railway bridges – a fact compensated by the spectacular circuit along the well-preserved city wall.

Conwy Castle's construction began in 1283 and was incredibly quick, taking just four and a half years. It is considered a masterpiece of medieval military architecture. With its eight solid round towers, it conveys the impression of an extremely well-fortified complex. Master builder James of Saint George (circa 1230 to 1309), a leading fortress architect, also oversaw the construction of Caenarfon and Harlech castles.

PONTCYSYLLTE AQUEDUCT

The potential offered by waterways was identified early on in Great Britain. And an outstanding example of this is the Pontcysyllte Aqueduct – the largest of its kind in this part of the world, measuring 307 m (1007 ft) in length and some 37 m (121 ft) in height. Soon after the inauguration of the aqueduct built by Thomas Telford and William Jessop between 1795 and 1805, its design, which features an elegant combination of cast-iron and stone elements, became the blueprint for similar structures all over the world. Celebrated as a 'waterway in the clouds', it is today still a unique experience to cross the aqueduct. This involves a boat ride down the cast-iron trough, which runs alongside a towpath where horses would once pull the boats. Visitors particularly enjoy seeing the trough's maintenance valve opened, prompting cascades of water to plunge into the River Dee.

PONTCYSYLLTE AQUEDUCT

The Pontcysyllte Aqueduct – designed as a navigable trough bridge crossing the Dee Valley in the northeast of Wales – is considered an engineering masterpiece, and has been listed as a UNESCO World Cultural Heritage site since 2009. The site also includes the adjoining canal. Boat rides here take place at a dizzying height of 40 m (131 ft) above the ground (below).

INDEX

PHOTOCREDITS / IMPRINT

MONACO BOOKS is an imprint of Kunth Verlag GmbH & Co KG
© Kunth Verlag GmbH & Co.KG, Munich, 2019

For distribution please contact:
Monaco Books
c/o Kunth Verlag GmbH & Co KG,
St.-Cajetan-Straße 41,
81669 München, Germany
Tel: +49.89.45 80 20 23
Fax: +49.89.45 80 20-21
info@kunth-verlag.de
www.monacobooks.com
www.kunth-verlag.de

Printed in Slovenia
Text: Christa Pöppelmann, Petra Dubilski, Reinhard Pietsch, Claudia Lensch
Translation: Sylvia Goulding